The Woman in Red

A Strategic Blueprint for Women to Rise Bold, Unshakable, Alive as Leaders

KEMI EMMANUEL

KEMI EMMANUEL PUBLISHING

Acknowledgements

I give all glory and honour to Almighty God, the ultimate source of my inspiration, wisdom, and strength. It is through His grace that I can write, create, and produce literature that I pray will be a blessing to the world.

I would like to sincerely acknowledge my husband and my children for their unwavering love and support. Thank you for standing by me, encouraging me, and allowing me the space to pursue this calling. Your belief in me means more than words can express.

My prayer is that God continues to keep you, guide you, and cover you in His grace. You are my world, and I am forever grateful for each of you.

Dedication

This book is dedicated to every hardworking woman who continues to rise, lead, and show up with purpose, despite the challenges, the pressures, and the unseen battles. You are the woman in red.

To the women who lead in boardrooms and in their homes, who pour into others while still finding the strength to pour into themselves, this is for you. Thank you for your resilience, your courage, and your unwavering commitment to your calling.

Thank you for showing up, not just in your work, but in your families, your communities, and in the quiet moments where your strength often goes unnoticed. You are seen.

You are valued. And you are making a difference.

Contents

Abstract

"The Woman in Red" is more than a leadership manual; it's a transformative journey into becoming a bold, purposeful leader who creates lasting impact. This book serves as your guide to unleashing your inner leader, combining practical strategies with spiritual wisdom and emotional intelligence. Through the metaphor of the woman in red, representing strength, passion, and purpose, you'll discover how to lead authentically in every sphere of life, from the boardroom to the living room.

Drawing from real-world experiences and timeless principles, this book empowers you to step into your full potential while maintaining balance and creating a legacy that inspires generations to come.

The woman in red is not defined by what she has, but by who she is. Even with little, she stands tall, rooted in her strength and fueled by her faith. Chains cannot hold her. Shackles cannot stop her. She forges ahead with courage, resilience, and determination.

The woman in red is a movement.

She is a force to be reckoned with.

She refuses to bow to imposter syndrome.

She pivots when the moment calls for it.

She carries a renewed mindset.

She burns with passion for her children, her partner, her work, and her calling.

Above all, she leads with love.

The woman in red is bold. She is unshakable. She is alive.

She is not just a woman—she is The Woman in Red.

Introduction: Why Red?

There she stood, resplendent in red, her presence commanding attention without uttering a word. As I watched this remarkable woman, navigate the conference room with grace and authority, I reflected deeply on what made her energy so magnetic, so unmistakably powerful. It wasn't just the vibrant crimson suit she wore - it was the way she wore it, with confidence, that seemed to radiate from within.

This encounter sparked a profound meditation on the symbolism of red and its deep connection to feminine leadership. Red - the color of life-giving blood, of passionate roses, of transformative fire. It represents both warning and warmth, danger and desire, power and protection. Just as a single spark can ignite a mighty flame, I realized that within every woman lies the potential for this same bold, life-giving leadership.

The Woman in Red isn't just about wearing a powerful color -

it's about embodying the qualities it represents. She is the leader who approaches challenges with calculated courage, the nurturer who fiercely protects what matters, the visionary who ignites positive change in her sphere of influence. She is the woman who has learned to harness both her strength and vulnerability, understanding that true power lies in the balance between them.

In my years as a mental health nurse, educator, author, and leader, I've witnessed countless women struggle with the weight of leadership expectations - often dimming their light to fit into predetermined moulds or burning out to prove their worth. This book emerges from these observations, from my journey of leadership across various domains, and from the urgent need for a new paradigm of female leadership.

What you hold in your hands is more than just a guide - it's a strategic blueprint for awakening the Woman in Red within you. Through these pages, we'll explore how to cultivate unshakeable resilience while maintaining authenticity, transform from passive thinking to bold action-taking, and create meaningful impact without sacrificing personal well-being.

Red has always been more than just a color.

It is fire.

It is blood.

It is love.

It is courage.

Red is not timid; it refuses to blend quietly into the background. It demands attention, evokes emotion, and carries weight. When a woman puts on red, something shifts. She stands taller and feels seen. She remembers her own strength. Red does not whisper; it declares. And so does the Woman in Red.The Woman in Red is not defined by her clothes, but by her presence. Resilient, compassionate, unshakable, and bold, she possesses remarkable strength. A leader, she knows precisely when to remain stationary and when to advance.

She is a mother, a businesswoman, a mentor, and a dreamer. She is any woman who dares to live on purpose, fully alive. This book is a blueprint for becoming that woman. Not by imitating anyone else, but by embracing the unique brilliance within you and daring to step into it without apology.Red reminds us of many things: fire, blood, roses, love, fireworks, warriors, the pulse, and legacy.

Each chapter uses red as a metaphor to uncover lessons about leadership, resilience, purpose, and impact. You will not only read stories and reflections, but you will pause to answer questions, write, and practice exercises that bring these lessons to life.Because here's the truth: you are already the Woman in Red. You carry within you the fire, the focus, the compassion, the resilience, the rhythm, and the legacy. This book will help you recognize, strengthen and unleash it. So, as you turn these pages, imagine slipping on that red dress, jacket, or scarf, not just as clothing, but as a symbol of courage, visibility, and strength.

This journey isn't about becoming someone else - it's about unleashing who you truly are. Whether you're leading in the boardroom or the living room, building a business or nurturing a family, this book will equip you with practical strategies and spiritual wisdom to rise bold, whole, and alive in your leadership.

Like the color red itself, true leadership isn't a destination but a dynamic force - one that brings warmth to those around us while maintaining healthy boundaries, that spreads influence while staying true to its source, that illuminates paths for others while burning bright and steady.

As you turn these pages, my prayer is that you'll recognize the Woman in Red already within you - the leader who knows how to draw boundaries while drawing others close, who understands that vulnerability can coexist with strength, who realizes that her greatest power lies not in perfection but in authentic presence.

The world needs your unique brand of leadership - your courage, your compassion, your conviction. It's time to rise, to shine, to lead with purpose and power. It's time to embrace the Woman in Red.

Let's begin.

CHAPTER ONE

Rising in Red: Bold by Nature, Built by Fire

In the depths of every woman lies an ember of leadership waiting to ignite into a magnificent flame of purpose and power. Like the bold brilliance of a red rose emerging from its bud, leadership unfolds from within, nurtured by experience and strengthened through challenges. The transformation from ember to flame mirrors every woman's journey into leadership - a path marked not by the absence of fear, but by the courage to rise despite it. Like a crimson thread woven through the tapestry of life, this inner fire manifests in countless ways, from the quiet strength of a mother guiding her children to the bold decisions of an executive steering her organization through change.

The woman in red is not necessarily the CEO of a company; she is the woman who is baked in fire but still comes out standing, refined like gold. The power to create impact doesn't live in titles or positions; it emanates from within. Many women find themselves in a position where they think, "I've achieved everything I thought I wanted, but somehow, I still feel like an impostor wearing a mask."

This echoes the silent battle many women face in leadership positions. Like a carefully constructed facade, we often build our external success while our internal foundation trembles with doubt. But here's what I've learned: true leadership isn't about wearing a mask; it's about wearing your authentic self with the boldness of a woman in red. Think about the woman in red for a moment. When she enters a room, she doesn't apologize for the space she occupies. She commands attention not through domination, but through the quiet confidence that radiates from within.

This is the leadership we're called to embody, one that balances strength with vulnerability, wisdom with warmth, and purpose with presence. A woman in red is courageous and bold. Few women have the courage to wear it, because they don't want to be seen; they want to just blend in. However, the woman in red knows that when she walks into a room, she stands out; she is noticed. Because red just catches your eye. But the woman who just wants to blend in, she doesn't do red. She just stays in the background, blending in with every color. She doesn't want to make a fuss or have people recognize her as a force. The woman in red knows that she doesn't even need to speak. Red speaks for her through her presence, making her stand out. In a picture, the red catches your eye.

Red announces her before she utters a word. It draws the eye, commands attention, and refuses to be ignored.

Like a flame in the dark, she stands out.

Like a rose among thorns, she is both tender and strong.

Even a sore thumb is noticed because it is red, different, and distinct.

The woman in red knows when to be different, and she embraces it. Her humility allows her to blend in when she chooses, but her drive ensures she rises when she must. She discerns when to speak and when silence is more powerful. She knows when to pause and when to push forward.

In my years as a mental health nurse, educator, and leader, I've witnessed countless women discover their inner flame - that distinctive spark that sets them apart as natural leaders. Leadership isn't merely about position or power; it's about the ability to inspire, guide, and transform. It's about recognizing that within each of us burns an eternal flame waiting to be fanned into its full potential.

Consider the story of Georgia, whose journey from self-doubt to self-assurance exemplifies the transformation many women need to experience on their path to leadership. Standing before her mirror in her crimson blazer, she faced more than her reflection -

she faced the culmination of fifteen years of experience, countless challenges overcome, and wisdom hard-won through service and dedication. Her story resonates with so many women who have questioned their capabilities despite proven track records of excellence.

Like Georgia, many of us have stood at the crossroads where timidity meets opportunity. Facing a crisis tests our leadership skills. These scenarios become a crucible where leadership abilities are refined and revealed. Sometimes, as a leader, you face limited resources and must create much with little. Take a busy ward: you are the nurse in charge. 2 staff members have called in sick, and you have 20 patients to look after. What do you do? Do you cower and hide in a cubicle or your office, or do you step forward and make a difference, claiming your power as a transformative leader unafraid to be on the front lines to protect your team? Yes, woman in red, this is a test of your ability to coordinate teams with precision, make swift, confident decisions, and maintain composure amid chaos.

This is what it means to be the woman in red - to recognize that leadership is not bestowed by titles but demonstrated through action. As a leader, when you embrace transformation, you stop questioning your position and start embracing your role. Therefore, it is imperative to illustrate a fundamental truth: true confidence emerges not from external validation but from an internal recognition of our inherent capabilities.

For Georgia, the red blazer became more than a garment; it became a symbol of her evolution. When she walked into work with her head held high, she carried with her the understanding that leadership is as much about presence as it is about position. Her team's response to this transformation, not just the change in her appearance but in her entire demeanor, reflects how authentic leadership radiates from within.

The woman in red knows that true confidence isn't about the absence of fear; it's about moving forward despite it, one of my favorite sayings (feel the fear but do it anyway). Like the deep red of a flame that burns brightest in darkness, our leadership qualities often shine most brilliantly when challenges test our resolve.

In this chapter, we'll explore the fundamental elements of becoming a bold and resilient leader. We'll examine how to harness our inner fire, transform challenges into opportunities, and build unshakable confidence through intentional practice and self-awareness. You'll discover that leadership begins with internal transformation - a journey of recognizing and embracing your natural abilities to guide, inspire, and create positive change.

As we delve deeper into these concepts, remember that leadership, like red itself, commands attention not through force but through its inherent power to inspire, influence and transform. Whether you're leading in the boardroom, the classroom, your community, or your home, the principles we'll explore will help you ignite and sustain your leadership flame.

Embracing Your Inner Fire: Understanding and Activating Natural Leadership Instincts

Like a flame that starts as a spark and grows into a powerful force, every woman's leadership journey begins with recognizing and embracing her inner fire. This innate leadership instinct, the quiet voice that urges us forward, the spark that ignites action, the warmth that draws others near - lies dormant in many until circumstances or choice fan it into full expression.

The story of Anita Garibaldi. This historical "Woman in Red" exemplifies this transformation. Ironically, in my research, I found one of the two known portraits of her painted in Rome, and she was arrayed in a red outfit. In 19th-century Italy, she demonstrated how embracing one's inner fire could ignite revolutionary change. She led troops, nursed the wounded, and inspired others, not because she was taught leadership, but because she recognized and activated the natural leadership instincts within her[1,2].

These leadership instincts manifest in various ways: the visionary thinking that sees possibilities where others see obstacles, the emotional intelligence that allows us to understand and motivate others, the courage to take calculated risks, and the resilience to persist through challenges. Like the deep crimson of a rose that blooms despite thorns, these qualities often emerge most powerfully in the face of adversity.

Psychological research confirms that self-awareness serves as the foundation for activating leadership potential[3]. Just as a flame needs oxygen to grow, our leadership instincts require conscious nurturing through reflection, mentorship, and purposeful action. Women who engage in regular self-reflection, whether through journaling, meditation, or meaningful dialogue with mentors, develop a deeper understanding of their strengths and areas for growth[3].

Consider how these instincts manifest in daily life: A mother mediating conflicts between siblings demonstrates natural conflict resolution skills. A team leader who navigates her group through organizational change demonstrates intuitive change-management abilities. A community volunteer who organizes resources for those in need displays innate strategic thinking. These scenarios illustrate how leadership instincts often emerge naturally in response to needs around us.

Activating your inner fire requires specific, actionable steps. Begin by identifying situations where you naturally take the lead - perhaps in family discussions, community projects, or workplace initiatives. Document these moments, noting what motivated you to step forward and what results you achieved. This practice builds self-awareness and confidence in your natural leadership abilities.

Create opportunities to strengthen these instincts through deliberate practice. Volunteer for projects that stretch your capabilities. Mentor others who are earlier in their journey. Seek challenges that make you uncomfortable. Remember, like a flame that grows stronger when tested by wind, your leadership abilities develop through challenges.

Build a network of support - other women leaders who can share experiences, offer guidance, and provide feedback. Like individual flames joining to create a more powerful fire, collective wisdom and support amplify individual potential. This network becomes crucial when facing obstacles or self-doubt.

Remember that embracing your inner fire doesn't mean you don't experience fear or uncertainty. Instead, it means recognizing these emotions as natural parts of the leadership journey while continuing to move forward. Like the ember that remains hot even when not visibly glowing, your leadership potential remains constant even when temporarily challenged.

Develop daily practices that nurture your inner fire. This might include morning reflection, regular exercise, or spiritual practices that center and ground you. Just as a flame needs constant fuel, your leadership energy requires regular renewal through self-care and personal development.

Most importantly, understand that your leadership style is uniquely yours. While you can learn from others, your most powerful impact will come from authentically expressing your natural instincts. Like the distinct shade of each red rose, your leadership signature carries its own beautiful and powerful hue.

As you progress on this journey, remember that embracing your inner fire is not a destination but a continuous process of growth and refinement. Much like gold refined through heat, every challenge and success contributes to the development of greater resilience and leadership capability. Your inner fire, once fully embraced and activated, becomes a beacon that not only lights your own path but illuminates the way for others to follow.

The Alchemy of Adversity: Converting Challenges into Leadership Gold

Like precious metal transformed by intense heat, adversity has a unique way of refining leadership qualities in women, turning challenges into golden opportunities for growth and impact. The process, much like the tempering of steel or the refining of gold, requires exposure to pressure, heat, and time - elements that test our resilience while revealing our true strength.

Indra Nooyi's journey at PepsiCo exemplifies this transformative process. As an immigrant woman in a male-dominated industry, she faced consistent skepticism and bias. Yet, like the phoenix rising from ashes, she transformed every "no" into fuel for innovation and every setback into a lesson in resilience[2]. Her experience demonstrates how adversity, when approached with strategic intent, becomes a catalyst for bold, transformative leadership.

The alchemy of adversity operates on multiple levels. At its core, it involves what psychologists call cognitive reframing - the ability to perceive challenges not as threats but as opportunities for learning and growth[2]. This mental transformation, supported by research from the Harvard Business Review, shows that women leaders who master this reframing process often develop greater confidence and more effective leadership capabilities [2.]

Reframing as a Tool for Resilience

Resilience is not just about "bouncing back." It's about how you interpret what happens to you and the story you choose to tell yourself in the face of setbacks. One of the most powerful tools for resilience is cognitive reframing, which shifts your perspective so that you see your own value, even in moments of rejection or loss.

Recognising Your Value

I once told a client, *"If you go for an interview and don't get the job, are you a failure? Or has the company lost something brilliant by not employing you?"* This is not denial; it is a mindset of worth. You are not diminished because someone else could not see what you bring.

The same principle applies in relationships. If a partner leaves, you have not lost everything. Instead, they have lost someone with depth, strength, and vulnerability. That is reframing: shifting the weight of loss away from yourself and placing it where it belongs.

As a leader, cognitive reframing recognizes your value. When you do this, you see your own value. You see, you bring something to the table, and if that is not valued, then it's their loss; that way, you don't cry and throw a pity party for yourself. This is not arrogance, but recognition of who you truly are as a woman in red.

Why This Matters for Resilience

When you reframe situations in this way, you build emotional armour. Disappointments no longer crush you, because you understand that your value is not determined by external decisions or other people's choices.

- Rejection becomes redirection.

- Loss becomes protection.

- Closed doors become signs of better openings.

This shift allows you to stand back up quicker, with less bitterness and more confidence, ready to try again.

The Woman in Red Mindset

Some may mistake this confidence for arrogance, but it is not. It is resilience. It recognises who you are and what you carry. The Woman in Red does not throw pity parties when things don't go her way. She reframes, she learns, and she moves forward with dignity.

Resilience means saying, *"If I was not chosen here, then it is their loss, not mine."* This mindset gives you the freedom to rise again, step into new opportunities, and lead without apology.

Ursula Burns' rise from poverty to becoming the first Black woman CEO of a Fortune 500 company at Xerox illustrates this principle in action. Like a flame that grows stronger when tested by wind, Burns used the adversity she faced as a platform to develop deeper empathy and drive systemic change[2]. Her story reminds us that our greatest challenges often contain the seeds of our most significant contributions.

The process of converting adversity into leadership gold requires specific, actionable strategies. First, develop a practice of meaning-making - finding purpose in your challenges[2]. This might involve journaling about difficult experiences, identifying the lessons learned, and connecting these insights to your larger leadership mission. Like the deep red of a rose that develops its richest hue through resistance to harsh conditions, your leadership qualities often deepen in the face of adversity.

Second, build and nurture strong support networks. Just as blood carries vital nutrients throughout the body, a robust network of mentors, peers, and supporters provides essential resources for navigating challenges[2]. These relationships offer perspective, wisdom, and emotional sustenance during difficult times.

Third, cultivate strategic adaptability. Like fire that changes form to consume different fuel, effective leaders learn to adjust their approaches when faced with obstacles[2]. This might mean developing new skills, exploring alternative pathways, or innovating solutions to seemingly insurmountable problems.

Fourth, harness the power of emotional intelligence and self-awareness. Adversity often serves as a crucible for developing a deeper understanding of ourselves and others. Through challenging experiences, we learn to manage our emotions more effectively and develop greater empathy for those we lead.

Finally, transform your experiences into compelling narratives that inspire and guide others[2]. As Maya Angelou wisely noted, "You may encounter many defeats, but you must not be defeated. In fact, it may be necessary to encounter defeats, so you can know who you are, what you can rise from, how you can still come out of it."[2]

The woman in red understands that adversity, like the refiner's fire, doesn't destroy - it purifies. Each challenge faced becomes another layer of strength, another shade of wisdom in her leadership palette. Whether navigating organizational change, balancing family responsibilities, or breaking through systemic barriers, she recognizes that today's tests are tomorrow's testimonies.

In the crucible of leadership, every challenge presents an opportunity for transformation. Like gold emerging from intense heat, more valuable and beautiful than before, women leaders who master the alchemy of adversity emerge stronger, wiser, and more capable of creating positive change in their spheres of influence[2]. The process isn't always comfortable, but like the refining of precious metal, the result is worth the heat of transformation.

Building Your Leadership Presence: Cultivating Unshakeable Confidence, Authentic Expression, and Visibility

Like a flame that illuminates darkness, true leadership presence radiates from within, casting light on paths forward while warming those around us with authentic energy. This inner radiance, much like the deep crimson of a rose in full bloom, develops not through imitation but through the careful cultivation of self-awareness, purpose, and unwavering confidence in one's unique gifts.

Research in leadership studies reveals that authentic leadership presence emerges from a deep alignment between our inner values and outer expression[1]. It's not about wearing a mask of authority, but allowing our true selves to shine through with clarity and conviction. Like the steady flame of a candle, this presence brings both light and warmth to those we lead.

Consider the journey of Christa, whose story exemplifies the power of authentic leadership presence. Initially hesitant to embrace her calling, she discovered that true confidence emerged not from mimicking others but from honoring her unique perspective and experiences[1]. Through conscious practice and self-reflection, she developed a leadership style that was both powerful and genuinely her own. Her transformation reminds us that leadership presence isn't about perfection - it's about showing up fully and authentically.

Cultivating unshakeable confidence requires specific, actionable practices. Begin with daily self-reflection - take time to acknowledge your strengths, examine your values, and align your actions with your core beliefs[1]. Like the deep roots that nourish a rose, this foundation of self-awareness supports the confident expression of leadership.

Develop your voice through intentional practice. Start in low-stakes situations - perhaps leading a family discussion or facilitating a team meeting. Pay attention to how you communicate, not just in words but in presence. Are you fully present? Does your body language reflect confidence? Like the gradual unfurling of a rosebud, leadership presence develops through patient, consistent practice.

Emotional intelligence plays a crucial role in authentic leadership. Research shows that leaders who understand and effectively manage their emotions while empathizing with others create stronger connections and inspire greater trust[1]. This emotional awareness, like the warmth of a flame, creates an environment where others feel safe to grow and contribute.

Resilience forms another cornerstone of unshakeable confidence. Just as a flame may flicker but doesn't extinguish in strong winds, resilient leaders maintain their presence through challenges[1]. Build resilience by practicing regular self-care, maintaining supportive networks, and viewing setbacks as opportunities for growth.

Authentic expression requires courage - the willingness to be seen, to speak truth, and to stand firm in your convictions. Like the bold red of a rose that cannot help but command attention, your authentic leadership presence will naturally draw others when you allow your true self to shine.

Practice strategic vulnerability. Share appropriate challenges and lessons learned, demonstrating both humanity and wisdom. This openness, when balanced with professional boundaries, creates deeper connections and inspires others to bring their authentic selves to their work.

Cultivate presence by being mindful of your physical presentation. While authentic leadership comes from within, how we present ourselves can either enhance or diminish our impact. Choose clothing and accessories that make you feel confident and aligned with your leadership identity. Like the woman in red, let your external presentation reflect your inner fire[1].

Remember that confidence, like a flame, requires fuel to sustain it. Regular learning, meaningful challenges, and celebrations of success all feed the fire of leadership presence. Seek opportunities to stretch your capabilities while staying true to your values and purpose.

Most importantly, understand that your leadership presence is uniquely yours. While you can learn from others, your greatest impact will come from authentically expressing your distinct gifts and perspectives. Like the unique pattern of a flame's dance or the particular shade of a rose's petals, your leadership signature carries its own beautiful and powerful energy.

As you continue developing your leadership presence, remember that this journey is ongoing. Each day brings new opportunities to align more deeply with your authentic self, to express your truth more clearly, and to impact others more powerfully. Like the woman in red, let your presence be a beacon of inspiration[1], lighting the way for others while remaining true to your own path. As we conclude this first chapter on rising bold, unshakable, and alive as leaders, let us reflect on the transformative journey we've explored. Like the deep crimson of a sunset that signals the promise of a new dawn, our exploration of leadership begins with recognizing the power that lies within each of us. The stories we've shared - from Georgia's evolution into confident leadership to the daily victories of women leading in their homes, communities, and organizations - illuminate the path forward for every woman ready to embrace her inner fire.

Red as Fireworks: Visibility & Boldness

Fireworks demand attention. Bursting with color, sound, and brilliance, they light up the night sky. They are not subtle, and they are not silent. They declare: *"I am here. I am meant to be seen."*

The Woman in Red carries that same spirit. She understands that leadership is not about hiding in the shadows or playing small.

It is about stepping into visibility with boldness, letting her light shine, and daring to occupy the space she has earned. I have seen countless brilliant and well-educated women who have achieved so much academically and, in their careers, cower under the weight of invisibility. My mission is to help them be seen and their voices be heard.

The Power of Being Seen

Too many women hesitate to step into visibility. They fear judgment, criticism, or the weight of expectations. That was me until I shifted my mindset. The Woman in Red mindset is bold. Mindset will be covered in the next chapter. When you hide, you deny others the gift of your brilliance.

Fireworks don't ask permission to shine. They don't wonder if the crowd will like them. They rise, they burst, they blaze, and in doing so, they inspire awe.

Visibility matters in leadership. Showing up boldly grants others permission to do the same. When you speak up, you shift the room. When you stand tall, you change the narrative for the women coming after you.

Breaking the "Invisible Barrier,"

Leadership studies show that women are often overlooked, not because they lack ability, but because they are invisible. Their work is solid, but their voices are quiet. Their results are strong, but their presence is hidden.

Consider **Oprah Winfrey**. She came from poverty and hardship, but she refused to remain invisible. She kept showing up until her voice and presence became a global platform.

Think about **Malala Yousafzai**. As a teenager, she spoke boldly about girls' education in Pakistan, even after surviving an assassination attempt. Today, her voice has reshaped international conversations about access to education.

Both women faced resistance, but both chose visibility. They became fireworks.

Boldness as a Strategy

Boldness is not arrogance; it is strategy. It is about positioning yourself where your voice can be heard, your ideas can be valued, and your influence can grow.

Fireworks are meticulously planned; they don't just explode randomly. They are designed for impact. The Woman in Red approaches boldness the same way. She knows when to rise, when to burst, and how to leave a lasting impression.

She invests in her visibility by:

- Speaking up in rooms where decisions are made.

- Sharing her expertise publicly, whether on stage, online, or in print.

- Networking strategically, building connections that elevate her presence.

- Dressing, speaking, and showing up in ways that reflect her confidence.

The Fear of Criticism

Every firework has noise. Some people will cheer. Others will cover their ears. Boldness attracts both applause and criticism. The Woman in Red accepts this reality. She knows that criticism is often the price of visibility. But she does not shrink because of it. She remembers fireworks are not meant to please everyone; they are meant to shine.

Real-World Fireworks

- **Michelle Obama**: Bold in redefining the role of First Lady, she used her platform to advocate for education, health, and equality, unapologetically being seen and heard.

- **Arianna Huffington**: Founder of *The Huffington Post* and *Thrive Global*, she became bold enough to challenge the way the world talks about success, introducing wellness and rest into the corporate conversation.

- **Serena Williams**: Her boldness was not just in her game, but in the way she embraced her identity as a strong Black woman in a sport dominated by others. Her presence itself was a statement of power.

These women remind us that being bold is not about perfection; it's about presence.

A Call to Rise and Shine

Like fireworks, your impact is meant to be seen. Don't hide your brilliance. Your voice is not for silence. Your presence is not an accident. So, rise, burst, and blaze. Be bold, be visible. Be the Woman in Red who lights up her world.

The fundamental elements we've examined - embracing our inner fire, transforming adversity into opportunity, and building authentic leadership presence - form the foundation of becoming the woman in red. These elements, like the intertwined threads of a tapestry, weave together to create a leadership style that is both powerful and distinctly feminine.

Leadership, as we've discovered, isn't confined to boardrooms or executive suites. It manifests in the quiet moments of parenting, in the strategic decisions of entrepreneurship, and in the daily acts of service that transform our communities. Like the varied hues of red that paint our world - from the subtle pink of dawn to the deep burgundy of dusk - leadership takes many forms, each uniquely beautiful and powerful.

The journey to becoming the woman in red is not a destination but a continuous process of growth and refinement. Like a flame that grows stronger with proper tending, your leadership capabilities will develop through conscious practice, resilience in the face of challenges, and unwavering commitment to your authentic expression.

As you move forward from this chapter, remember that your leadership journey begins with embracing your inner fire - that divine spark that sets you apart and calls you to greater purpose. Whether you're leading a team, nurturing a family, building a business, or serving your community, let your light shine with the boldness of crimson, the warmth of a flame, and the life-giving power of blood coursing through veins.

Carry with you the understanding that true leadership emerges not from perfection but from authenticity. Like the rose that blooms regardless of thorns, your leadership will flourish when you embrace both your strengths and vulnerabilities. Let each challenge refine you, like gold in the fire, emerging more valuable and beautiful than before.

As we transition to exploring the mindset shifts necessary for leadership success in the next chapter, hold fast to these foundational truths: You are built for leadership. Your experiences, both triumphs and challenges, have prepared you for this journey. And like the woman in red who commands attention not through force but through presence, your authentic leadership will naturally draw others to your light.

Take a moment now to reflect on your own leadership journey. What inner fire has been waiting to be ignited? What challenges are ready to be transformed into opportunities? How will you let your unique leadership presence shine? The path forward awaits, illuminated by the bold, unshakable spirit of the woman in red - the leader you were always meant to become.

Reflection

1. Where in my life have I been playing small or hiding, even though I know I should step forward?

2. What fears hold me back from being more visible—fear of criticism, failure, or judgment?

3. Who inspires me as a bold, visible leader? What can I learn from her?

4. What platforms or spaces could I step into, to increase my visibility?

5. What does "being bold" look like for me in the next season of my life?

Practical Exercises

Visibility Audit: Write where you are currently visible (e.g., work meetings, social media, community). Then, identify one new platform or space where you can show up more boldly.

Bold Move Challenge: This week, take one bold step you've been avoiding, whether it's speaking up in a meeting, posting your work online, or asking for an opportunity.

CHAPTER TWO

The Mindset Shift: Restructuring and rewiring your brain for success

Like tempering steel in fire, transforming your mindset requires deliberate exposure to challenges that strengthen your leadership capacity. The journey of rewiring your brain for success begins with an understanding that every thought pattern you've developed can be reshaped, just as surely as a sculptor molds clay into a masterpiece. Just as every masterpiece begins with a single brushstroke, the journey of rewiring your mindset for leadership excellence starts with understanding the power of conscious transformation. The path to becoming the woman in red - bold, resilient, and unstoppable - requires more than mere positive thinking; it demands a fundamental restructuring of how we perceive ourselves and our capabilities.

This transformation mirrors refining precious gold, where intense heat transforms raw potential into something brilliant and valuable. The fire that shapes us may come in many forms - professional challenges, personal setbacks, or moments of self-doubt. Like the unwavering flame that refines gold, these experiences strengthen rather than diminish our leadership capacity.

Many women are like a lady I want to call Rosie. Rosie is a health-care Department Director whose journey exemplifies the power of intentional mindset transformation. Like many women stepping into leadership roles, she initially struggled with an inner dialogue that questioned her readiness and capability, something we all know now to be "imposter syndrome". Her vision board, filled with aspirations and possibilities, stood in stark contrast to the limiting beliefs that threatened to hold her back. She needed a mindset reset.

Yet, through deliberate practice and conscious effort to rewrite her internal narrative, Rosie discovered what many successful women leaders eventually learn: that our mindset is not fixed but a garden we can actively cultivate. Each morning, she would pause in her car, taking five precious minutes to visualize herself as the leader she aspired to be. This wasn't mere daydreaming; it was active mental rehearsal, a practice of programming her brain for success.

The transformation she experienced demonstrates a fundamental truth about leadership mindset. It's not about becoming someone different, but about unleashing the potential that already exists within. Rosie documented her "leadership wins" and consciously reframed challenges as opportunities for growth. Rosie literally rewired her brain's response to leadership demands.

As we delve deeper into this chapter, we'll explore practical strategies for this kind of mindset transformation. Like the woman in red who stands bold and unafraid, you'll learn how to harness the power of neuroplasticity - your brain's remarkable ability to form new neural pathways - to build the mental foundation for exceptional leadership.

You'll discover how to identify and dismantle limiting beliefs that may be holding you back, replace self-doubt with strategic thinking, and develop the mental resilience that characterizes truly impactful leaders. We'll explore specific techniques for transforming passive thinking into decisive action, ensuring your leadership potential isn't just understood in theory but expressed in practice.

The journey of mindset transformation isn't always comfortable - like the refining fire that shapes precious metal, it often requires us to face our fears and challenge our assumptions. But remember, the woman in red isn't defined by the absence of fear, but by her ability to move forward despite it, letting the flames of challenge temper rather than consume her courage.

The Power of Mindset–The Woman in Red Has a Mindset that is Intentional

Mindset is a set of beliefs that shape how we think, act, and what we believe. The Woman in Red knows one powerful truth: mindset shapes destiny. Her mind is set on achieving the goals she decides on, and nothing, not delay, setbacks, or opposition, can easily shake her focus.

I remember being at a meeting where a lady was about to buy a raffle ticket at the same time as me. She turned to me and confidently declared, "I'm going to win this."

Curious, I asked, "Why do you think you're going to win? I'm here too, and I'm also buying a ticket." She smiled and said, "Because I decided before I even came here that I was going to win. The last time I came, I told myself the same thing, and I won. This time, I've already purposed in my mind that I will win again."

I walked away thinking, " Let the best person win. But in truth, she had something I didn't have, a winner's mindset. And yes, she won the raffle. I congratulated her, but I also learned a valuable lesson that day: the right mindset can open doors to your goals.

Mindset in Action

Not long after, I was in another raffle situation;would win nothing this time; it was my colleague who was buying a ticket. I decided not to purchase a ticket because I believed I would win nothing.

Now, this was a limiting belief which I never knew I carried until that day. But then I remembered that earlier incident. I realized I was speaking with a loser's mentality. So, I changed my approach. I bought the ticket and decided, really decided, that I was going to win.

When the prizes were announced, it looked like I had won nothing. Others around me were getting excited, and disappointment crept in. But then I caught myself and thought, No. I am the Woman in Red. I will win.

I whispered a prayer, fixed my thoughts on victory, and told myself, Your prize is coming. And then it happened, the next raffle called was mine! Not only that, but my prize turned out to be the better one.

The Mindset Difference

That day reminded me of a powerful truth: When your mind is set on doing something, it fuels, prepares and guides you. It keeps you from giving up when things don't go your way at first.

The Woman in Red knows that: "Winners never quit. Quitters never win".

She doesn't stop at the first "no" or back down when success takes time. She stays in the race until she crosses the finish line, because her mind is already there before her feet arrive.

The Woman in Red: Bold Leadership, Lasting Influence, and the Power of Showing Up

I once encountered three women who deeply stirred something within me. The first was a poet. She shared a few verses, raw, powerful, rich with emotion. I was moved. Her words had rhythm, depth, and beauty, but she was scared. Scared to share her voice with the world. "What if no one cares?" she asked. Then I met a businesswoman, an entrepreneur with a brilliant product, a clear vision, and remarkable skill. But she'd paused everything. She was terrified of networking. "I don't think I belong in those rooms," she whispered. Then came the woman who was ready to give up. She had poured her heart into creating content, posting videos, and writing a book. But no one seemed to listen. "What's the point?" she sighed. However, she stated that one person replied, commented, and said, "Thank you. This helped me." And everything changed.

This is the power of limiting beliefs. The power to limit you as a leader and put a ceiling on your achievements. If you can see the impact your leadership and bold steps have on even one person, you can break that glass ceiling and bloom like a rose.

Because sometimes, all it takes is one. Showing Up Intentionally isn't about reaching the masses; it's about reaching the one. When we withhold our gift because we fear judgment, silence, or rejection, we're not just protecting ourselves. We're denying the world of something life-giving.

Someone could find healing in that poet's language. That entrepreneur's idea might lead to someone's significant achievement. The story of that discouraged writer could be a beacon for those facing hardship. This is what it signifies to be The Woman in Red.

The Intent Blueprint

The Woman in Red is Intentional in her mindset. When I think of The Woman in Red, I think of fire. Fire spreads intentionally and has a purpose. When we use it for cooking, its role is clear: to prepare a meal to perfection. The fire's responsibility is to ensure the food is cooked well. The cook's responsibility is to add the right ingredients, spices, seasoning, oil, and herbs to make the dish not just edible, but exceptional. Even something as simple as rice, bland on its own, transforms when cooked with care and a pinch of salt.

The woman in red is an outstanding leader who doesn't stumble into greatness; she plans for it and makes bold moves with clarity and purpose. Every step she takes is aligned with her values, vision, and God-given assignment. She knows that intentional living is the bridge between dreams and destiny. She is not swayed by distractions, delays, or doubts. This leads her to invest her time, energy, and resources in what matters most. It is important to understand that nothing extraordinary happens by accident.

Are you ready to live intentionally, to rise bold, unshakable, and alive? The journey starts with a single decision, and now is the moment to make it.

The Cooking Analogy for Leadership and Life

If you are a Woman in Red, or aspire to be, you lead with purpose and intent, just as a meal has a clear end goal to nourish the eater. You must be intentional about where you're going and what you want to achieve. Like fire contained under a pot, your energy and focus must be contained within your goals. Fire without boundaries causes destruction, but fire with purpose transforms ingredients into nourishment.

The mother who wakes her children is intentional; her aim isn't just to get them out of bed, but to prepare them to be leaders of the future.

The leader at work is intentional about building and nurturing a team, knowing when to add the right "ingredients" to encourage growth and unity.

The woman in ministry is intentional about the impact she wants to make, whether to change lives, inspire transformation, or guide others into their destiny.

Why Intent Matters

In life, even in the courtroom, intent changes everything. It determines outcomes. If something was intentional, the result and the judgment are different. The same applies in leadership, parenting, ministry, and personal growth: your outcomes are shaped by your intent.

My Red Dress Experiment

Recently, I wore my red dress intentionally, not just for style, but to observe how it would make me feel and how others would respond.

The results were remarkable. An older lady at the bus stop where I was standing complimented me and even helped me with bus times. She looked at me with admiration and complimented me on my outfit. Subsequently, on the bus, she gave me the opportunity to get ahead of her, treating me with such dignity.

During this experiment, as I proceeded towards my destination, another person stopped me on the street and said, "You look absolutely beautiful." Those words lifted my confidence instantly. I had been late for the event I was attending and had been debating whether to go, but the compliments shifted my mood entirely. By the time I arrived at the event, I walked in with boldness, spoke confidently, and made valuable connections. That is what the Woman in Red does; she radiates confidence, presence, and purpose.

Be Intentional Like Fire

As a woman in red, you lead like fire. Fire spreads warmth, light, and essence. She spreads influence, inspiration, and transformation. To be a Woman in Red, you must:

- Be intentional with your actions.

- Have a clear goal and keep your "flame" contained within it.

- Add the right ingredients at the right time.

- Lead with emotional intelligence and purpose.

Some of us are impulsive, I know I can be, but even my impulses are now intentional. They are guided by my mission and where I'm going.

- Like fire, I want my work to be done well.

- Like fire, I want my excellence to draw people to me.

- Like fire, I want my message to spread, igniting hearts and minds.

The Woman in Red is Not Ordinary:

- She is fire, bold, warm, and alive.

- She is blood, flowing with life, resilience, and purpose.

- She is a rose, beautiful, even surrounded by thorns.

- She is passion, presence, and power

To show up as the Woman in Red is to lead, even when it's hard, influence even when the audience is small, wear boldness like a crown, not because you're fearless, but because you know the cost of staying silent. You carry oxygen, and oxygen brings life. So, when you don't show up, someone somewhere is gasping for air.

Sometimes You Just Need a Transfusion

Let's be real, every strong woman runs low sometimes, even the woman in red. The fear creeps in, doubts get loud. You feel invisible, feel the life draining out of you, energy slowly slipping away, losing iron, and the dulling of zeal. The passion that once blazed fades under the weight of overwhelm and burnout. You wake up knowing you have responsibilities to carry, people to lead, and decisions to make, but you feel empty, unequipped, and stretched beyond capacity.

The Woman in Red understands that strength is not in pretending to have it all together, but in recognizing when she needs a transfusion. Transfusion is not weakness; it is wisdom. It is the intentional act of restoring what has been lost. It may look like learning a new skill to sharpen your edge, seeking guidance from a coach or mentor who can help you see clearly again, stepping into networking spaces that reignite your vision, or investing in professional platforms that equip you for growth.

This is how you infuse life back into your bloodstream and restore your strength, your clarity, your focus. The Woman in Red does not wait until she is completely depleted; she refuels, she recharges, she realigns. And in doing so, she rises again as the leader she was always called to be, strong, focused, and full of life.

You are not invisible.

Neuroplasticity and Leadership: Understanding Your Brain's Capacity for Change

The human brain, like the transformative power of fire, holds remarkable potential for change and growth. Just as a flame can be carefully tended to illuminate darkness, our neural pathways can be intentionally reshaped to enhance our leadership capabilities. This fascinating ability of our brain to reorganize itself - known as neuroplasticity - offers women leaders a powerful foundation for transformation and growth[8].

Like the deep crimson petals of a rose that unfold gradually to reveal their full beauty, our brain's capacity for change doesn't happen overnight but through consistent, purposeful action. Research shows that women often possess enhanced neural circuitry for emotional intelligence, empathy, and interpersonal communication - qualities that are increasingly recognized as crucial for effective leadership [4,5,7].

Consider Sarah, a mental health nurse who transformed herself from a quiet team member into a confident ward manager. Initially overwhelmed by the prospect of leading a large team, she discovered that leadership abilities weren't fixed traits but could be developed through deliberate practice[8]. We discussed what it means to lead and identified her innate leadership qualities. She turned out to be one of the best leaders in the organization and was recognized for her management and leadership style. By consistently engaging in new challenges and learning opportunities, she literally rewired her brain's response to leadership demands.

The science of neuroplasticity reveals that every time we learn something new or practice a skill, we create and strengthen neural pathways[8]. This process mirrors how a flame spreads and grows stronger when given proper fuel and attention. For women leaders, this means that qualities like decisiveness, strategic thinking, and emotional resilience can be cultivated through intentional practice.

Just as blood carries vital nutrients throughout our body, bringing life and strength to every cell, our brain's neural networks carry information that shapes our thoughts, emotions, and behaviors. By understanding this process, we can intentionally create experiences that foster positive leadership traits. Research shows that activities like mindfulness meditation can alter the structure of brain regions responsible for emotional processing and decision-making[67].

Practical strategies for harnessing neuroplasticity in leadership include regular reflection on leadership experiences, seeking constructive feedback, and engaging in continuous learning. These practices strengthen neural circuits involved in self-awareness and decision-making[8], much like how regular exercise strengthens muscles.

For mothers and family leaders, understanding neuroplasticity offers insight into how to create positive change at home. A mother's brain undergoes significant neuroplastic changes during pregnancy and early parenthood, enhancing capabilities for empathy and multitasking - skills that translate powerfully into other leadership contexts[5].

The woman in red understands that, like the ember that can reignite into a powerful flame, her brain's capacity for growth and change remains vital throughout life. She embraces challenges as opportunities for neural growth, knowing that each experience shapes new pathways for success. Whether leading in the boardroom or nurturing relationships at home, she leverages her brain's remarkable plasticity to develop and refine her leadership capabilities.

To actively engage your brain's capacity for change, consider implementing these evidence-based practices:

- Engage in regular mindfulness meditation to enhance emotional regulation and decision-making[6,7]

- Seek new learning experiences that challenge your current capabilities[8]

- Practice reflective journaling to strengthen neural pathways for self-awareness

- Build strong social support networks to enhance resilience and adaptive stress responses[9]

Like the process of tempering steel in fire, each challenge and learning experience you embrace helps reshape your neural pathways, strengthening you and making you more resilient. The woman in red knows that her leadership journey is not about becoming someone different, but about unleashing the potential that already exists within her brain's remarkable capacity for change[8].

Remember, just as a single spark can ignite a powerful flame, small, consistent actions in developing your leadership skills can lead to significant transformation through the power of neuroplasticity[8]. Your brain is constantly ready to adapt and grow - it's up to you to provide the experiences that will shape it into the leadership powerhouse you envision.

Identifying and Dismantling Limiting Beliefs: The Power of Conscious Thought Restructuring

Like a flame that illuminates shadows, our journey to leadership excellence begins with shining light on the dark corners of our minds where limiting beliefs live. These self-imposed barriers, though powerful, are not permanent fixtures of our psyche but learned patterns waiting to be transformed through conscious awareness and deliberate restructuring.

Just as the deep crimson of a rose emerges from a tightly closed bud, our potential often remains constrained by beliefs formed through past experiences, cultural conditioning, or past setbacks. Research shows that these limiting beliefs commonly manifest as imposter syndrome, reluctance to pursue promotions, or self-sabotaging behaviors that hold women back from fully stepping into their leadership power[10].

Consider limiting beliefs, such as the belief that a quiet nature makes one unsuitable for leadership. This limiting belief can form when outspoken personalities dominate leadership positions, discouraging the individual from pursuing advancement opportunities. Through deliberate self-reflection and journaling, an individual can recognize how this belief contradicts evidence of their capabilities, such as building trust with clients, mentoring junior staff, and implementing innovative protocols.

Breaking Free from Limiting Beliefs

I once worked with a client who carried heavy limiting beliefs. She said to me, *"They don't care. They will not do anything about it. It's always like this."*

Her words reflected defeat before the situation had even unfolded. She had convinced herself that the outcome would always be negative, no matter what.

After listening to her, I gently challenged her perspective. I said, *"Why don't you give them a chance? Instead of believing nobody cares, what if you reframe it to, maybe they haven't received your application? Maybe someone made a mistake, or something went wrong."*

That small shift in language changed everything. She moved from a place of hopelessness to possibility. As we worked together on restructuring her mindset, she felt lighter. Her spirit calmed. Peace returned.

Limiting Beliefs and Peace

The Woman in Red understands that peace of mind is power. When you allow limiting beliefs to dominate your thinking, you lose that peace. Limiting beliefs don't just shape your expectations; they shape your energy. They can steal your passion, undermine your confidence, and hold you hostage in a life smaller than the one you're meant to live.

Limitless Thinking

Reframing is the path to freedom. When you challenge limiting beliefs, you make space for possibilities. You allow your mind and spirit to consider new outcomes, better opportunities, and greater solutions. This is the mindset of the Woman in Red; she refuses to let limiting beliefs make her small. She chooses peace, power, and the limitless life she was born to lead.

The process of dismantling limiting beliefs requires the same patience and precision as tempering steel in fire. Just as a blacksmith carefully applies heat and pressure to transform raw metal into something stronger, we must apply conscious awareness and structured techniques to reshape our thought patterns. This transformation begins with three key steps:

- Mindful observation of our automatic thoughts, especially during challenges or setbacks

- Systematic examination of the evidence supporting or contradicting our beliefs

- Deliberate reframing of limiting statements into empowering alternatives

Dr Carol Dweck's research on mindset demonstrates that individuals who believe their abilities can be developed (growth mindset) consistently outperform those who view their capabilities as fixed. This scientific understanding provides hope - our limiting beliefs, though deeply ingrained, can be rewired through intentional practice.

For mothers and family leaders, this process often begins at home. A mother who believes she must choose between career success and family engagement can learn to reframe this limiting belief into an empowering truth: her leadership skills enhance her parenting, while her nurturing capabilities enrich her professional impact.

The woman in red understands that, like the ember that can reignite into a powerful flame, her potential isn't limited by past beliefs but expanded by present choices[10]. She approaches the dismantling of limiting beliefs with the same precision and care she would apply to any crucial leadership task:

- Regular journaling to track recurring negative thoughts

- Seeking feedback from trusted mentors and peers

- Practicing positive affirmations that align with her leadership vision

- Engaging in small "behavioral experiments" that challenge limiting assumptions

Like blood that carries vital oxygen to every cell, new empowering beliefs nourish every aspect of leadership. When we consciously restructure our thoughts, we don't just change our minds - we transform our actions, our impact, and ultimately, our legacy.

The process of dismantling limiting beliefs often reveals that what we perceived as weaknesses can become unique strengths. The same sensitivity that made us question our leadership capability might be the very quality that allows us to build strong, trust-based teams. Thoughtful strategic planning might develop from the caution that made us hesitate.

Remember, just as a single spark can ignite a powerful flame, a single shift in belief can catalyze tremendous leadership growth.

The woman in red knows that her journey of transformation isn't about becoming someone different, but about unveiling the leader she's always been, hidden beneath layers of limiting beliefs[10].

Through conscious thought restructuring, we learn to see ourselves not as we fear we are, but as we truly can be - bold, capable, and ready to lead with both strength and authenticity. Like the refining fire that shapes precious metal into something more valuable, dismantling limiting beliefs transforms us into leaders who can light the way for others.

The Power of Thought: The Woman in Red Chooses Differently

William James wisely noted, *"The greatest weapon against stress is our ability to choose one thought over another."*

This truth is both simple and transformative. As leaders, we often face internal battles that are far more intense than external pressures, limiting beliefs, self-doubt, and the quiet voice of imposter syndrome that whispers, *"You're not enough."* But the Woman in Red understands something powerful: thoughts are not facts; they are choices. And what you choose to think shapes how you lead, how you show up, and how you rise.

Reframing: Replacing What Limits You

Thought replacement, also known as reframing, is the deliberate act of interrupting a limiting belief and choosing a more empowering truth.

When the thought says:

- *"I'm not qualified enough,"* → the Woman in Red replaces it with: *"I am growing, learning, and becoming more than capable."*

- *"I don't belong in this room,"* → she reframes it to: *"I bring value that only I can offer."*

- *"What if I fail?"* → She shifts it to: *"What if I succeed, and this is my moment?"*

You cannot always control your first thought, but you can always choose your next one.

Breaking the Grip of Imposter Syndrome

Imposter syndrome thrives on unchallenged thoughts. It feeds on comparison, perfectionism, and the fear of exposure. But the Woman in Red does not allow those thoughts to settle unchecked. She questions them, reframes them, and replaces them. She understands that confidence is not the absence of doubt; it is the decision to move forward despite it.

Building Resilience Through Thought Mastery

Resilience is not just about enduring external challenges; it is about mastering your internal dialogue.

Every time you replace a limiting belief with an empowering truth, you strengthen your resilience muscle. You train your mind to support you rather than sabotage you.

Over time, this practice transforms you:

- You respond instead of reacting

- You rise instead of retreating

- You lead with clarity instead of confusion

Resilience is built in the quiet moments when you choose courage over fear in your thinking.

The Woman in Red Chooses Her Thoughts

The Woman in Red is intentional. She does not allow her mind to drift into negativity unchecked. She guards her thoughts as she guards her purpose.

She knows that what flows through her mind will eventually flow through her leadership, her words, and her actions.

So, she chooses wisely.She reframes boldly.She rises consistently.

A Call to Think Differently

Today, pause and listen to your thoughts. What are you telling yourself? Are those thoughts building you up, or breaking you down? If they are limiting you, replace them. If they are draining you, reframe them.

Because your greatest weapon is already within you, the power to choose your next thought.

Creating Success Rituals: Daily Practices for Mental Strength and Resilience

Like the steady flame that transforms raw materials into refined gold, success rituals forge mental strength and resilience through daily practice and unwavering commitment. When performed consistently, these intentional habits become the foundation upon which unshakeable leadership is built, much as the deep roots of a rosebush support its brilliant crimson blooms.

Just as blood carries vital oxygen to every cell in our body, daily success rituals nourish our mental and emotional capacity, ensuring we remain strong and resilient in the face of leadership challenges. Research from the Center for Healthy Minds demonstrates that consistent mindfulness practices change the brain's emotional circuitry, enhancing our ability to regulate stress and maintain clarity under pressure [1].

I had the opportunity to observe a mental health nurse manager who enhanced her leadership effectiveness by adopting deliberate daily practices. Each morning, before the demands of managing her unit began, she would spend ten minutes in mindful reflection - a ritual that research shows can significantly decrease stress hormones and enhance focus[1]. This simple yet powerful practice became her anchor, allowing her to approach each day's challenges with renewed clarity and purpose as she reflected on the previous day's activities. She identified what went well and what needed improvement. She considered what needed improvement and would set at least one small goal for the day to make the changes she deemed necessary.

The woman in red understands that, like the carefully tended flame that never extinguishes, mental strength requires constant nurturing through deliberate practice. Drawing from evidence-based research, successful women leaders often incorporate these essential rituals into their daily routines: ·

Morning Mindset Activation: Begin each day with spiritual connections such as prayer, intentional breathing, meditation, or reflection.

- Strategic Goal Setting: Identify top priorities and set micro-goals for the day[2]

- Physical Empowerment: Incorporate movement or "power poses" to boost confidence and cognitive function[2]

- Gratitude Practice: Record three specific things to be grateful for, building optimism over time

- Evening Reflection: Review accomplishments and lessons learned, planning adjustments for tomorrow

Like the process of tempering steel, these rituals grow more powerful with consistent practice. Harvard Business Review reports that women executives who maintain morning routines that incorporate reflection, planning, and exercise consistently report higher well-being and career satisfaction[2].

For mothers and family leaders, these rituals take on additional significance. A mother's morning ritual might include both personal centering and family connection, creating a powerful foundation for both home and professional leadership. As James Clear notes, "You do not rise to the level of your goals. You fall to the level of your systems."[3] This truth applies equally to leading in the boardroom or nurturing family relationships.

The science of neuroplasticity reveals that our brains literally reshape themselves through repeated practice. Each time we engage in our success rituals, we strengthen neural pathways that support resilience and leadership capabilities. Like an ember that can reignite into a powerful flame, these strengthened neural connections allow us to access our best selves even in challenging moments.

To build your own success rituals, start small and build gradually. Research shows that layering one new ritual at a time creates more lasting change than attempting wholesale lifestyle changes. Consider these practical steps:

Choose one morning ritual to begin with, perhaps five minutes of mindful breathing

Track your consistency using a journal or habit-tracking app

Adapt the ritual to fit your unique schedule and energy patterns

Celebrate small wins and adjust as needed

Like the deep crimson rose that blooms more vibrantly with proper care, your leadership presence will strengthen through these daily practices. Remember, as William James wisely noted, "The greatest weapon against stress is our ability to choose one thought over another." Through conscious ritual-building, you develop this ability to choose thoughts and actions that serve your highest leadership potential.

The woman in red knows that her mental strength, like a well-tended flame, requires both fuel and protection. She understands that daily rituals aren't just tasks to complete but sacred practices that forge her leadership capacity. Whether leading teams, nurturing families, or building communities, these rituals become the foundation of her unshakeable presence and lasting impact.

By consistently implementing these evidence-based practices, you create a reservoir of mental strength and resilience that, like the life-giving properties of blood, nourishes every aspect of your leadership journey. Your daily rituals become the crucible in which your leadership potential is refined, allowing you to emerge stronger, more focused, and ready to illuminate the path for others. As we conclude this transformative journey through mindset shifts and mental rewiring, let us remember that, like the steady flame that refines gold, our leadership capacity grows stronger through conscious cultivation and unwavering commitment. The process of restructuring our thoughts and rewiring our brains for success isn't merely about changing what we think - it's about transforming how we show up as leaders in every sphere of our influence.

Like the deep crimson rose that blooms more vibrantly with proper care, the woman in red emerges from her mindset transformation with renewed clarity and unstoppable determination. Through understanding neuroplasticity, dismantling limiting beliefs, and establishing powerful success rituals, she creates an unshakeable foundation for leadership excellence.

Moving from self-doubt to strategic thinking reminds us that transformation is possible through intentional practice and conscious rewiring of our thought patterns. The woman in red approaches challenges not as obstacles but as opportunities for growth, using each experience to strengthen her leadership capacity.

The practices and principles we've explored in this chapter - from understanding our brain's remarkable capacity for change to establishing daily success rituals - provide a practical framework for your own leadership transformation. Like blood that carries vital nutrients to every cell, these mindset shifts nourish every aspect of your leadership journey, from professional excellence to family relationships.

Remember that this transformation, like the process of tempering steel in fire, requires patience and persistence. The woman in red understands that lasting change comes not from sporadic effort but from consistent, intentional practice. Each small step in rewiring your mindset builds upon the last, creating a powerful foundation for bold, authentic leadership.

As you move forward, carry with you the understanding that your leadership potential, like an ember waiting to ignite, holds infinite possibilities. Through conscious thought restructuring and daily practice, you can unleash this potential, emerging as the leader you're truly meant to be - bold, resilient, and unstoppable.

Let the practices we've explored become part of your daily leadership ritual, transforming how you think, decide, and act. Like the flame that both illuminates and transforms, your renewed mindset will light the way not only for your own journey but for those you lead and influence.

The woman in red knows that true leadership begins in the mind, but its impact extends far beyond personal transformation. As you step into each new day with your transformed mindset, remember that you carry within you the power to inspire, influence, and create lasting change in every sphere of your influence.

Embracing these mindset shifts isn't just about personal growth - it's about creating a legacy of bold, authentic leadership that inspires others to rise and shine in their own unique way. Like the brilliant red of dawn that pushes back darkness, your transformed leadership mindset will illuminate paths for others to follow.

As we close this chapter, remember that every great leader's journey begins with a single thought transformed. Your mindset transformation journey has just begun, and the possibilities that await you are as limitless as the sky above. Step forward with confidence, knowing that you carry within you everything needed to lead with boldness, purpose, and unwavering strength.

Reflection

1. What limiting belief have I been holding onto that is preventing me from stepping fully into my leadership potential, and where did it originate from?

2. If I replaced that belief with one rooted in confidence and purpose, how would my decisions, actions, and leadership style change?

3. What is one bold action I can take today that challenges my current mindset and proves that I am capable of more?

Chapter Three

Leading with Heart: Mastering Emotional Intelligence

The most powerful leadership tool isn't found in strategic plans or management theories - it resides in the heart's capacity to understand, connect, and inspire. Like the deep crimson heart of a rose that nurtures its outer petals to bloom, a leader's inner emotional intelligence shapes the beauty and effectiveness of their external influence. The journey of mastering emotional intelligence in leadership begins with an understanding that our greatest impact often stems from our ability to connect deeply with others while maintaining our own emotional equilibrium. Just as a crimson heart pulses with life-giving vitality, emotional intelligence keeps the rhythm of effective leadership beating strong and steady.

In the intricate dance of leadership, beauty emanates not just from external presentation but from the depth of understanding we bring to every interaction. The woman in red knows that her influence flows from an authentic integration of inner wisdom and outer grace - like the perfectly balanced petals of a red rose, each aspect enhancing the other's strength.

Emma's story illustrates this delicate balance beautifully. As a senior nurse manager facing resistance to change, she discovered that technical expertise alone couldn't bridge the gap between protocol and people. Her journey from focusing purely on practical implementation to embracing emotional awareness transformed not just her leadership approach, but the entire dynamic of her ward. Through this experience, Emma embodied the essence of the woman in red - someone who leads not just with competence, but with heart.

Emotional intelligence in leadership isn't just about being nice or maintaining harmony. Like the controlled power of a flame, it requires careful cultivation and conscious application. It means developing the ability to read the emotional undercurrents in a room while maintaining your own centered presence. It's about recognizing when to turn up the heat and when to provide warmth and nurturing support.

As we explore the four pillars of emotional intelligence -

self-awareness, self-management, social awareness, and relationship management - we'll discover how each element contributes to creating leadership presence that's both powerful and authentically beautiful. We'll examine practical strategies for developing these capabilities while maintaining the delicate balance between professional effectiveness and personal well-being.

Just as red symbolizes both passion and power, emotional intelligence in leadership combines warmth with strength and empathy with excellence. This chapter will guide you through cultivating emotional mastery that enables you to lead with both heart and wisdom, creating an impact that resonates deeply with those you lead while maintaining your own emotional well-being.

The journey to becoming a woman who leads with heart requires courage to look within, willingness to grow, and commitment to authentic expression. Like the deep red of a sunset that transforms the entire sky, your emotional intelligence can change the atmosphere of any environment you enter. As we delve into this crucial aspect of leadership, remember that true beauty in leadership flows from the alignment of inner wisdom with outer expression - just as the woman in red embodies both grace and power in perfect harmony.

Red as Love: Leading with Compassion

Red is the color of love, the heartbeat of humanity, the sign of sacrifice, the mark of compassion. Love is not weakness; it is strength wrapped in gentleness. It is the Woman in Red's secret power, the invisible force that drives her leadership, nurtures her family, and strengthens her community.

The world often confuses leadership with domination, control, or authority. But true leadership flows out of love, which serves, uplifts, and makes sacrifices. The Woman in Red leads with both strength and tenderness. She understands that love is not a soft option, but the most powerful foundation a leader can build upon. Organisations now understand this love and have called it EQ, Emotional Intelligence.

The Four Pillars of Emotional Intelligence in Leadership

- Self-Awareness,

- Self-Management,

- Social Awareness,

- Relationship Management

The journey through emotional intelligence in leadership is like the carefully controlled flame of a torch - it must be tended with awareness, managed with skill, understood with depth, and shared with purpose. For the woman in red, these four pillars form the foundation of her leadership presence, allowing her to shine brightly while nurturing the flames of potential in others.

Self-awareness, the first pillar, acts as the inner flame that illuminates our understanding. Like a candle casting light inward, it reveals our emotional landscape, strengths, limitations, and values[11] [12] [14] [15]. Research by Daniel Goleman demonstrates that leaders with high self-awareness make better decisions and create more positive team environments[11]. This inner knowing allows us to recognize when our flame burns too hot with anger or too low with doubt, enabling us to adjust our approach accordingly.

Consider the story of Dr Sarah, a Managing director at a major product firm. When faced with implementing significant organizational changes, she first took time to examine her own emotional responses to the transition. Through regular journaling and mindful reflection[11], she recognized her anxiety about the change was influencing her communication style with her team. This self-awareness allowed her to adjust her approach, leading to more effective implementation and stronger team engagement. It is important to be aware of your own emotions and how major changes affect them. Sometimes, having to oversee and manage such change can create varying levels of anxiety, which can then be translated into poor team management and emotional dysregulation.

Self-management, the second pillar, represents our ability to tend our inner fire with skill and purpose. Like controlling a flame that must neither be extinguished nor rage out of control, self-management requires careful regulation of our emotional responses [11] [12] [14] [15]. This pillar enables us to remain calm under pressure, adapt to changing circumstances, and maintain our course toward goals despite obstacles[11 12].

Social awareness, the third pillar, extends our light outward, allowing us to read the emotional climate of a room and understand the needs of others[11 12 14 15]. Like the way a single flame can illuminate an entire space, social awareness helps us recognize the unspoken concerns, aspirations, and dynamics within our teams and organizations[13]. This empathetic understanding becomes crucial in times of change or crisis.

Patricia, a nursing director, exemplifies the power of social awareness. During a challenging hospital merger, she noticed subtle signs of anxiety among her staff through their body language and interaction patterns. She acknowledged these concerns openly and created safe spaces for dialogue. She maintained team cohesion and performance during the transition by taking time out to lead with compassion, recognizing potential sources of staff unrest and addressing them before they became problems.

Relationship management, the fourth pillar, represents our ability to use emotional intelligence to forge strong connections and inspire others[11 12 14 15]. Like the way a flame can spread from one torch to another without diminishing its own light, effective relationship management allows us to develop and nurture meaningful professional connections while maintaining appropriate boundaries[13].

These four pillars work in harmony, each strengthening the others[11] [14] [15]. When we're self-aware, we can better manage our responses. When we understand others, we can build stronger relationships. Together, they create a foundation for leadership that is both powerful and nurturing.

For the woman in red, mastering these pillars means developing specific practices:

- Regular reflection through journaling or meditation to enhance self-awareness

- Stress management techniques for maintaining emotional equilibrium

- Active listening skills to deepen social awareness

- Intentional relationship-building through mentorship and support

Like the deep red of a rose that maintains its beauty while protecting itself with thorns, these practices allow us to lead with both strength and sensitivity. They enable us to navigate complex emotional landscapes while maintaining our own well-being and effectiveness.

The mastery of emotional intelligence isn't a destination but a continuous journey of growth. As Goleman's research shows, these skills can be developed and refined through conscious practice and experience[11] [15]. Each challenge becomes an opportunity to deepen our emotional intelligence, much like how pressure and heat transform raw materials into precious gems.

For the woman in red, emotional intelligence becomes her signature strength - not a soft skill, but a powerful force that enhances every aspect of her leadership. It allows her to lead with both heart and wisdom, creating an impact that resonates deeply with those she guides while maintaining her own emotional equilibrium.

Through these four pillars, we learn to lead not just with authority, but with authentic emotional wisdom. Like the steady flame of a torch, this kind of leadership illuminates paths for others while maintaining its own bright, unwavering light.

Cultivating Inner Beauty: Aligning Values, Actions, and Leadership Style

Like a precious gem refined by intense heat, inner beauty in leadership emerges through the conscious alignment of our deepest values with our daily actions. The woman in red understands that true leadership radiance comes not from external adornments but from the consistent expression of authentic principles through every decision and interaction. This alignment creates a magnetic presence that draws others toward our light, much like moths to a flame.

The journey of cultivating inner beauty begins with deep self-reflection. Just as a jeweler must understand the inherent properties of each stone before cutting and polishing, leaders must first gain clarity about their core values. Research by Kouzes and Posner reveals that values serve as our internal compass, guiding our decisions and framing our interactions with the world[16]. When we align our leadership style with these values, we create an authentic presence that others can trust and follow.

Maya is a school headteacher at a major metropolitan school. Early in her leadership journey, she struggled with the disconnect between her natural empathetic approach and the more directive style she thought leadership required. Through careful reflection and journaling, she discovered that her greatest strength lay in leading from a place of authentic compassion. By aligning her leadership style with her core value of nurturing others' growth, she transformed her school's culture. The result was decreased staff turnover and the development of a team that began to embody the same value-driven approach. She developed empathetic leaders in the various departments, and that trickled down to all other staff members.

EQ as Strength

EQ is a leader's ability to lead from a place of love, which is often portrayed as fragile or sentimental, but love has the strength to forgive, to reconcile, to endure. It outlasts conflict and bridges divides. The Woman in Red knows that while authority may command compliance, only love inspires loyalty and legacy. Her love is not naïve; it is discerning. It does not ignore boundaries but builds them. She leads with love, not to be liked, but to leave others better than she found them. The Woman in Red recognizes that leadership is not about titles or applause, but about service. She is strong enough to stand firm, yet tender enough to see the needs of those around her.

As a clinical lead at a major hospital, I wrote my first book, "Love Made This Happen", while leading a challenging team. However, I was able to create cohesion within the team by leading from a place of love and showing empathy to the challenges staff were facing at the time. Staff turnover was high, and morale was low. My key focus was on building a cohesive team and a culture of care; after all, we were nurses, trained to care and be compassionate. Why could we not model this with our team? That was my question at the time. Like the woman in red, my aim was to bring life to the team and create a flow of oxygen that did not choke but improved the quality of life within the department.

Compassion does not make you weak; it makes you unforgettable.

Love in leadership requires balance. Too much harshness and people wither. Too much softness and people drift. The Woman in Red finds the rhythm, firm but compassionate, strong but tender. Like a mother who disciplines in love, or a shepherd who guides with both rod and staff, she balances strength with care. Her leadership is like a heartbeat, steady, life-giving, and essential.

A Call to Lead with Love

The greatest leaders are remembered not for their power, but for their love. Biblically, I refer to Jesus, whose core message was love. He was a leader who did not build an empire, but built lives, and His love transformed the world.

So too, the Woman in Red does not measure her success only by numbers or accolades, but by the lives she has touched with love. Your leadership, whether in the home, workplace, or community, will only last if it is rooted in love. Lead with compassion, courage, and love.

The Power Within

Cultivating inner beauty requires regular practices that reinforce this alignment[16]:

- Daily reflection on decisions and their alignment with core values

- Regular feedback sessions with team members to ensure actions match intentions

- Mindful observation of how our leadership style impacts others

- Continuous learning through reading and studying other women leaders[17]

Like the deep red heart of a rose that retains its vibrancy even as the outer petals age, inner beauty in leadership deepens with time and experience. It's about developing a leadership presence that, like the steady flame of a torch, provides both warmth and illumination to those around us.

The woman in red recognizes that inner beauty manifests differently in various contexts - from the boardroom to the family dinner table. As a mother, she might express it through patient guidance and consistent modeling of values. As a team leader, it might be reflected in ethical decision-making and empathetic communication. In each role, the alignment between values and actions creates an authentic leadership presence that others naturally trust and respect.

Transforming values into consistent action requires courage and commitment. Like the process of tempering steel in fire, it often involves challenging moments that test our resolve. However, each time we choose to act in alignment with our values, especially when it's difficult, we strengthen our inner beauty and leadership presence.

The practice of vulnerable leadership, as highlighted in contemporary leadership research, shows that acknowledging our humanity while maintaining our principles creates deeper connections and more resilient teams[18]. Like the red rose that bears both soft petals and protective thorns, we can lead with both gentleness and strength.

To cultivate lasting inner beauty in leadership:

- Regularly assess the alignment between your stated values and daily actions[16]

- Seek feedback from trusted colleagues about how your leadership style impacts others

- Create opportunities for open dialogue about values and their practical application

- Develop practices that nurture your spiritual and emotional well-being

Remember that inner beauty in leadership, like a well-tended flame, requires constant attention and care. It's not about achieving perfection, but about maintaining consistent alignment between who we are and how we lead. When our values, actions, and leadership style align, we create a presence that, like the woman in red, combines strength with grace, power with compassion, and authority with authenticity.

This alignment becomes crucial during challenging times. Like blood that carries vital nutrients throughout the body, our inner beauty nourishes our leadership presence even in moments of stress or uncertainty. It provides the foundation for resilient leadership that can weather any storm while maintaining its essential character and influence.

The Art of Empathetic Leadership: Building

Stronger Teams Through Emotional Connection

Like the warmth of a carefully tended hearth, empathetic leadership creates an environment where teams can flourish and grow. The woman in red understands that true leadership power flows not from authority alone, but from the ability to forge genuine emotional connections that inspire trust, loyalty, and collective achievement. Just as a single flame can ignite many others without diminishing its own light, empathetic leadership multiplies strength through understanding and authentic connection.

Research from Harvard Business School's Leadership Initiative demonstrates that leaders who master emotional connection drive superior team performance, innovation, and employee retention[19] [20]. Like the life-giving properties of blood flowing through veins, empathy carries vital energy throughout an organization, nourishing every interaction and decision with understanding and insight.

When implementing significant organizational changes, it is important to recognize that your team's resistance stems not from the changes themselves but from unaddressed fears and concerns. Rather than pushing forward with authority alone, you can create safe spaces for dialogue and actively listen to each team member's perspective. Through this empathetic approach, you can transform resistance into collaboration, ultimately achieving better outcomes than initially projected.

The art of empathetic leadership requires specific practices that build emotional connection[19]:

- Active listening that demonstrates genuine interest and understanding

- Creating psychological safety where team members feel valued and heard

- Celebrating authenticity and encouraging others to bring their whole selves to work[19]

- Mentoring and championing others, particularly those facing unique challenges[19]

Like the deep red petals of a rose that protect its heart while displaying its beauty, empathetic leadership balances vulnerability with strength. It requires courage to open ourselves to others' experiences while maintaining appropriate boundaries and professional standards.

The impact of empathetic leadership extends beyond the workplace into every sphere of influence. As mothers, we use emotional intelligence to guide our children through challenges. As community leaders, we build bridges through understanding and compassion. In each role, empathetic leadership creates connections that strengthen the fabric of our relationships and communities.

A department's culture can be transformed through empathetic leadership. A leader must know if staff are burning out and stress levels are rising. Implementing regular check-ins that go beyond professional updates to address emotional well-being demonstrates empathy. Consider creating a "care circle" where team members can safely share their challenges and support one another in a safe space; this could be termed "reflective practice". I had to implement this in my role as clinical lead, enabling staff to air their views without feeling biased or judged. The result was not just improved morale but also enhanced patient care outcomes. This meant an emotionally supported team brought their best selves to work.

For the woman in red, empathetic leadership means developing specific skills[19]:

- Emotional awareness that allows us to read unspoken needs

- Compassionate communication that validates others' experiences

- Boundary setting that protects our energy while maintaining connection

- Cultural sensitivity that honors diverse perspectives and experiences

Like the steady flame of a torch that provides both warmth and light, empathetic leadership combines nurturing support with clear direction. It creates an environment where team members feel both challenged and cared for, driving them to achieve their highest potential while feeling valued and understood.

The practice of empathetic leadership requires regular self-reflection and intentional development[19]. Just as a flame must carefully maintain its strength, our capacity for emotional connection needs consistent attention and care. This might involve regular meditation practices, seeking feedback from team members, or engaging in professional development focused on emotional intelligence.

Through mastery of empathetic leadership, the woman in red creates teams that are not just high-performing but deeply connected and resilient[19]. Like the way blood carries both strength and healing throughout the body, her emotional intelligence infuses her organization with vitality and purpose, creating lasting impact through the power of authentic connection.

In conclusion, as we explore leading with heart and mastering emotional intelligence, we remember that our leadership presence, like the steady flame of a torch, requires both inner radiance and outward warmth. The woman in red understands that true beauty in leadership emanates from the alignment of emotional wisdom with purposeful action, creating an impact that transforms both us and those we lead.

Through this journey, we have witnessed how emotional intelligence transformed not just the leadership approach but the entire culture of an organization. Let us remember that when we lead with heart - balancing technical expertise with emotional awareness - we create environments where both people and performance can flourish. Like the deep crimson of a rose that derives its vibrancy from a healthy core, leadership excellence flows from emotional mastery.

The four pillars of emotional intelligence - self-awareness, self-management, social awareness, and relationship management - provide a framework for developing leadership presence that combines strength with sensitivity. Just as blood carries vital nutrients throughout the body, these pillars nourish every aspect of our leadership, from decision-making to team building, from crisis management to the celebration of success.

Cultivating inner beauty through the alignment of values, actions, and leadership style creates an authentic presence that others naturally trust and follow. Like the process of tempering steel in fire, this alignment often requires us to withstand challenging moments that test our resolve. Yet each time we choose to act within our values, especially when it's difficult, we strengthen our leadership presence and inspire others to do the same.

The art of empathetic leadership teaches us that true power flows not from authority alone, but from the ability to forge genuine emotional connections. Like a single flame that can ignite many others without diminishing its own light, empathetic leadership multiplies strength through understanding and authentic connection. When we lead with both heart and wisdom, we create teams that are not just high-performing but deeply connected and resilient.

As you move forward in your leadership journey, remember that, like the woman in red, your strength lies not just in what you do but in how you touch the hearts and minds of those you lead. Let your emotional intelligence be the flame that illuminates paths for others while maintaining its own bright, unwavering light. In mastering the delicate balance between heart and mind, between strength and sensitivity, between inner beauty and outer impact, you become not just a leader but a beacon of inspiration for others to follow.

In the next chapter, we'll explore how to transform this emotional mastery into decisive action, moving from heart-centered understanding to bold, purposeful leadership that creates lasting impact. Just as the woman in red combines grace with power, we'll discover how to harness our emotional intelligence to drive meaningful change while staying true to our authentic selves.

Reflection

How do I currently show emotional intelligence in my leadership, family, or community?

Where have I withheld compassion out of fear of being seen as "weak"?

Who in my life needs more compassion from me right now?

What balance of strength and tenderness do I need to cultivate in my leadership?

If love and compassion are the legacy I leave, what actions today will reflect that legacy?

Chapter Four

The Colors of Influence: Action Over Intention, Impact over analysis and Timidity to Triumph

In the vibrant spectrum of leadership, the boldest hues belong to those who dare to move beyond intention into action, painting their vision across the canvas of possibility. Like the deep crimson of a sunset that transforms the entire sky, a woman's influence grows not through careful contemplation alone, but through the courage to act decisively and purposefully. The journey from contemplation to action marks the defining moment where leaders distinguish themselves from dreamers. For many women, the path to decisive leadership is often clouded by societal expectations of timidity and excessive caution. Yet, the woman in red understands that true influence emerges not from endless analysis, also known as analysis paralysis, but from courageous action grounded in wisdom and experience.

I know people might call me impulsive, but I call it action. I don't just dream, I take action to make my dreams a reality. Like the steady pulse of lifeblood flowing through veins, leadership requires constant movement and purposeful flow. When we remain still, analyzing every possible outcome or waiting for perfect conditions, we risk becoming stagnant - much like a flame deprived of oxygen. The woman in red recognizes that every moment of hesitation is a missed opportunity to make an impact, inspire change, and demonstrate the power of decisive leadership.

"Perfectionism is the killer of Action,"

Standing Out Boldly

In a garden full of green leaves and muted colors, it is the rose that stands out. And so, it is with the Woman in Red. She knows that standing out is not arrogance; it is alignment with who she was created to be.

Many women shrink in fear of standing out. They worry about being judged, misunderstood, or attacked. But the Woman in Red understands that her uniqueness is not a weakness; it is her gift. Like the rose, she dares to be seen.

When we talk about the woman in red as a bold leader, it's about recognizing that every step she takes to share her voice breathes life into someone else's world. For the poet who's been hiding her poetry, the entrepreneur who's been too hesitant to network, or the new content creator about to give up, each of these women has a unique gift. By stepping up and owning that bold, vibrant identity, you're not just leading yourself; you're influencing and uplifting others. If you imagine your voice as oxygen someone else needs to breathe, it helps you see that holding back keeps that gift from the world. That's where you can find the courage to keep going and truly shine.

The Scent of Influence

A rose not only catches the eye but also leaves a fragrance behind. The Woman in Red is remembered not only for what she looks like, but for the atmosphere she creates. Her kindness, her wisdom, her strength, all leave behind a fragrance that lingers long after she has gone. Her leadership is neither silent nor loud for attention. It is fragrant, subtle, yet undeniable.

As a leader, you might sometimes face a defining moment when your organization needs to rapidly adapt its service delivery model during a crisis. Some leaders will spend their time analyzing data. Now, I am not saying this is bad; sometimes it is necessary to give a clearer picture of what could be going on. Sometimes, as a leader, you need to recognize when swift action is necessary and act boldly. Rapid training sessions, clear communication channels, and personal demonstrations of the new procedures might be required. Decisive leadership not only improves outcomes but also inspires the team to embrace change with confidence. They don't see bureaucracy; they see ownership and take ownership of the process enough to get things done quickly. It is imperative to understand that impact comes not from perfect planning, but from courageous action backed by experience and expertise. True leadership isn't about having all the answers, but about having the courage to move forward and adjust course as needed.

The transformation from timidity to triumph doesn't happen overnight - it's forged in the crucible of challenges, tempered by experience, and strengthened through deliberate practice. Like the gradual building of a fire from ember to flame, each small act of courage builds upon the last, creating a sustainable source of warmth and light that others can gather around and draw strength from.

In this chapter, we'll explore the practical frameworks and emotional intelligence strategies that enable women to move beyond analysis paralysis into purposeful action. We'll examine how to harness influence effectively while maintaining authenticity and discover how calculated risk-taking can bridge the gap between good intentions and meaningful impact. The woman in red understands that her power lies not in perfect planning, but in purposeful action - in the courage to step forward when others step back, to speak up when silence feels safer, and to lead with conviction even when the path ahead isn't fully illuminated.

From Analysis to Action: Breaking Through Decision Paralysis

The journey from analysis to action is like the transformation of a flame from ember to roaring fire - it requires both the spark of decision and the oxygen of courage to truly ignite. For many women leaders, the tendency to over-analyze can become a subtle form of self-sabotage, dim their natural brilliance and prevent their light from fully illuminating the path ahead[1]. Yet, like the woman in red who harnesses the power of her inner fire[2], breaking through decision paralysis requires embracing both wisdom and boldness.

Consider the vital nature of blood flowing through our veins - it cannot pause to analyze its path; it must move continuously to sustain life. Similarly, effective leadership requires a steady flow of decisions and actions. When we allow ourselves to become trapped in the cycle of endless analysis, we risk stagnating not only our own growth but also the development of those who depend on our leadership[1].

The transformation from analysis to action begins with understanding that perfection is not the goal - progress is. Like the natural spread of a flame that adapts to its environment, effective decision-making requires flexibility and trust in one's instincts. The woman in red recognizes that every decision carries both opportunity and risk, but she chooses to focus on the potential for growth rather than the possibility of failure.

To break through decision paralysis, consider implementing the 80/20 (the Pareto Principle): focus on the critical 20% of information that drives 80% of outcomes. This approach prevents getting lost in minutiae while maintaining the essence of thoughtful leadership. Set clear decision deadlines, recognizing that time is a valuable resource that cannot be recovered once spent on excessive analysis.

Create a personal decision-making framework that honors both analytical thinking and intuitive wisdom. Start by identifying your core values and non-negotiable principles - these become your guiding lights when navigating complex choices. Then, establish clear criteria for different types of decisions, recognizing that not every choice requires the same depth of analysis.

For instance, when facing decisions about your children's education or family dynamics, trust your maternal instincts while gathering essential information. In professional settings, leverage your experience while remaining open to innovative approaches. The key is finding the balance between thorough consideration and timely action[1].

Practice the art of incremental boldness - start with smaller decisions to build your confidence muscle. Like a flame that grows stronger with each piece of fuel it consumes, your decision-making abilities will strengthen with each choice you make. Celebrate these small victories, recognizing that each decisive action builds momentum toward larger transformations.

Remember that breaking through decision paralysis isn't about eliminating analysis altogether - it's about finding the sweet spot between thoughtful consideration and purposeful action. Like the deep red rose that knows exactly when to unfurl its petals, trust your inner wisdom to guide your timing.

Establish a support network of other women leaders who can serve as sounding boards and accountability partners. Sometimes, simply verbalizing our analysis helps us recognize when we've crossed the line from prudent consideration into paralyzing overthinking. These relationships can provide both a mirror for reflection and a spark for action.

Most importantly, recognize that decision paralysis often stems from a fear of imperfection rather than a lack of capability[1]. The woman in red understands that her power lies not in making perfect decisions, but in making progress through purposeful action[2]. She knows that, like the refining fire that transforms raw materials into precious gold, each decision - whether it leads to success or learning - refines her leadership capacity and strengthens her ability to create meaningful impact.

The Impact Matrix: Measuring and Maximising Your Leadership Influence

Like the steady pulse of a heart pumping life-giving blood through the body, leadership influence flows through every interaction, decision, and relationship we nurture. The Impact Matrix serves as a compass for the woman in red, helping her measure and maximize her influence across all spheres of life - from the boardroom to the living room, from community initiatives to personal relationships. Just as blood carries vital nutrients to every cell, effective leadership influences, nourishes, and strengthens every aspect of our professional and personal ecosystems.

The Impact Matrix combines quantitative and qualitative measures to provide a comprehensive view of leadership effectiveness[21] [22] [23].

Like the multiple facets of a perfectly cut ruby, it reflects different dimensions of influence –

- business outcomes

- team engagement

- personal credibility

- organizational change

- social impact[21] [23] [24].

Each dimension requires its own kind of attention and nurturing, much like a garden that needs different care for its various plants to thrive.

Danielle is a healthcare executive who transformed her department's performance by applying the Impact Matrix principles. Rather than focusing solely on traditional metrics like patient throughput and cost efficiency, she expanded her measurement framework to include team well-being, mentorship effectiveness, and community health outcomes.

The Mayo Leadership Impact Index validated her approach, showing strong correlations between this holistic leadership style and reduced staff burnout, increased professional fulfilment, and improved patient care outcomes[24].

The woman in red understands that influence, like fire, requires both fuel and careful tending. The Impact Matrix provides structure for this process through several key dimensions:

- Business Outcomes: Measuring tangible results and organizational growth[22]

- Team Engagement: Assessing motivation, retention, and empowerment[22]

- Personal Influence: Evaluating credibility, visibility, and advocacy[21]

- Organizational Change: Gauging adaptability and culture-shaping capability

- Social Impact: Measuring community contribution and partnership effectiveness[21,23,24]

Like the deep crimson petals of a rose that unfold layer by layer, leadership influence develops through intentional practice and careful cultivation. The Impact Matrix helps identify areas where our influence can grow stronger, much like a gardener knowing which plants need more attention to reach full bloom.

In the home environment, the Impact Matrix principles apply just as powerfully. Consider how you measure your influence as a parent or partner - not just through daily tasks accomplished, but through the quality of relationships built, the values instilled, and the personal growth fostered in family members. These same dimensions of influence that shape corporate success can transform family dynamics.

The woman in red recognizes that maximizing influence requires regular assessment and adjustment. Like the careful monitoring of vital signs, the Impact Matrix provides crucial feedback on the health and effectiveness of our leadership[21][24]. It helps us identify when to turn up the heat of our influence and when to temper it with patience and understanding.

To implement the Impact Matrix effectively, consider these practical steps:

- Regular Self-Assessment: Schedule quarterly reviews of your influence across all dimensions

- Feedback Integration: Actively seek and incorporate input from those you lead and influence[24]

- Goal Alignment: Ensure your influence objectives support both organizational and personal growth

- Impact Measurement: Track both quantitative metrics and qualitative outcomes[21][22]

Remember that influence, like the flow of life-giving blood, must remain dynamic and adaptable. The woman in red understands that leadership impact isn't about wielding power, but about creating positive transformation in every sphere she touches. Through careful application of the Impact Matrix, she can ensure her influence remains both powerful and purposeful, like a well-tended flame that provides both light and warmth to all it reaches.

As Simon Sinek wisely noted, "Leadership is not about being in charge. It's about taking care of those in your charge."[22] The Impact Matrix helps ensure we fulfil this sacred responsibility with intention and effectiveness. Like the deep red of a sunset that transforms the entire sky, your leadership influence has the power to create lasting changes in every life you touch.

Triumph Over Timidity: Building Courage Through Calculated Risk-Taking

Like a flame that grows stronger with each challenge it faces, courage in leadership is not about the absence of fear, but about the wisdom to harness it productively. The woman in red understands that timidity, much like an untamed fire, can either consume us or be channeled into a force that illuminates paths and warms hearts. Through calculated risk-taking, she transforms natural caution into strategic boldness, much as intense heat transforms raw gold into precious jewelry.

The journey from timidity to triumph begins with understanding that courage, like the steady flow of lifeblood through our veins, requires constant movement and renewal. Research consistently shows that women often face unique challenges in overcoming timidity, particularly in leadership roles, where assertiveness may be viewed through different lenses than those of their counterparts[1]. However, like the deep crimson rose that pushes through thorny barriers to bloom, women leaders can cultivate courage through intentional practice and calculated risk-taking.

Consider the story of Indra Nooyi, former CEO of PepsiCo, who demonstrated how calculated risk-taking can transform both an organization and an industry. When faced with changing consumer preferences, she made the bold decision to diversify PepsiCo's portfolio toward healthier options, despite significant initial resistance. Her courage to challenge the status quo, grounded in careful analysis and strategic thinking, ultimately led to substantial growth and industry leadership.

Confidence Building

:

From Timidity To Triumph

The transformation from timidity to triumph requires a systematic approach, much like how a skilled artisan works with precious metals. Begin by identifying your 'courage zones' - areas where you naturally feel confident - and gradually expand from there. For instance, if you're comfortable leading family discussions but hesitate in professional settings, start by applying your home-tested leadership strategies in smaller work situations.

Remember that courage, like fire, grows stronger when properly fed and tended. Start with small risks - perhaps speaking up in a meeting or proposing a new initiative in your community group. Each success builds confidence for larger challenges, such as advocating for organizational change or launching a new business venture.

As a mental health professional, I've observed how fear often masquerades as prudence, keeping capable women from embracing their full leadership potential. The key is learning to distinguish between genuine caution and self-limiting timidity. Like the difference between a controlled flame that provides warmth and an untamed fire that destroys, understanding this distinction helps us channel our natural caution into productive risk-taking.

In parenting and family leadership, calculated risk-taking might mean allowing children more independence while maintaining appropriate safety nets, or having difficult but necessary conversations about family dynamics. These domestic applications of courage often translate powerfully into professional settings, demonstrating how leadership skills flow naturally between different life domains.

The woman in red understands that triumph over timidity isn't about eliminating fear - it's about developing the wisdom to act despite it[2]. Like blood that carries both oxygen and antibodies throughout the body, courage carries both the energy for bold action and the wisdom for calculated decisions. Through consistent practice and strategic risk-taking, she builds a legacy of courage that inspires others to rise beyond their own limitations.

Remember the words of Eleanor Roosevelt, who said, "You must do the thing you think you cannot do."[1] This isn't a call to reckless action, but rather an invitation to calculated courage - the kind that transforms timidity into triumph, one bold decision at a time. Like the refining fire that turns raw gold into precious jewelry, each calculated risk you take refines your leadership capacity and strengthens your ability to create meaningful impact. As we conclude this chapter on moving from analysis to action, from timidity to triumph, let us remember that like the deep crimson sunset that transforms the entire sky, our influence as leaders grows not through endless contemplation, but through purposeful, decisive action. The woman in red understands that while thorough analysis has its place, true impact emerges from the courage to move forward, to take calculated risks, and to trust in both experience and intuition.

Through our exploration of how to break through decision paralysis, we've discovered that leadership, like the steady flow of lifeblood, requires constant movement and renewal. Just as blood carries vital nutrients throughout the body, your decisions carry transformative potential to every area of your influence - from the boardroom to the family room, from community initiatives to personal relationships.

We've examined the Impact Matrix, learning how to measure and maximize our influence across multiple dimensions of leadership. Like the facets of a perfectly cut ruby, each aspect of our leadership - whether professional achievement, team development, or family nurturing - requires its own unique care and attention to shine at its brightest.

In our journey from timidity to triumph, we've discovered that courage, like fire, grows stronger with each challenge it faces. Remember that calculated risk-taking isn't about eliminating fear, but about developing the wisdom to act despite it. Like the process of refining gold, each bold decision you make strengthens your leadership capacity and adds to your value.

As you move forward from this chapter, carry with you the understanding that action is the bridge between intention and impact. Let your leadership flame burn bright and steady, illuminating paths for others while warming hearts with your authentic presence. Remember that you, like the woman in red, are built for this - forged through experience, strengthened by challenges, and refined by purpose.

The journey from analysis to action is ongoing, but with each step forward, you demonstrate the power of decisive leadership. Like the deep red rose that knows exactly when to unfurl its petals, trust your inner wisdom to guide your timing. Your influence, like a well-tended flame, has the power to transform not only your own path but the trajectories of all those you lead.

As you close this chapter, reflect on the areas where you've been hesitating and choose one bold action to take tomorrow. Remember, the woman in red doesn't wait for perfect conditions - she creates them through purposeful action and unwavering commitment to growth. Your time to act is now, and your impact awaits.

Let your leadership light shine bold and bright, illuminating paths and inspiring others to rise beyond their own limitations. For in the end, it is not our analysis that changes the world - it is our courage to act, to lead, and to create meaningful impact in every sphere we touch.

A Call to Bloom

Your life may be surrounded by thorns, criticism, hardship, and pain, but do not let them stop your bloom. Stand tall. Shine brightly. Release your fragrance. Thorns are part of your story, but they do not define your beauty.

Be the rose. Be the Woman in Red who blooms boldly among thorns.

Practical Exercises

Thorn & Bloom Journal: Write three challenges (thorns) you have faced. For each, note one strength (bloom) it developed in you.

Bloom Boldly Practice: Identify one area where you've been shrinking back. Take one step this week to show up fully, whether it's speaking up, sharing your work, or stepping into visibility.

Fragrance of Influence: Ask three trusted people what quality of yours they admire most. Note their answers and reflect on how you can spread that "fragrance" more intentionally.

CHAPTER FIVE

A Pillar at Home and Beyond: Navigating Leadership Across Life's Domains

Leadership, like the steady flame of a torch, illuminates not just one path but radiates across all aspects of a woman's life, from the intimate spaces of home to the broader arenas of professional and community influence. Just as the deep red roots of a mighty tree nourish every branch, a woman's leadership presence strengthens and sustains all the domains she touches. The journey of leadership spans every domain of a woman's life, weaving threads of influence into a tapestry of impact at home and in the professional sphere. Like the unwavering commitment of a lighthouse keeper, women leaders must maintain their brilliance across multiple domains, ensuring their light reaches every corner where guidance is needed.

Just as a ruby catches and reflects light from every facet, effective leadership requires us to shine in multiple directions simultaneously. Whether guiding children through life's challenges, managing teams through organizational change, or nurturing ageing parents through their golden years, the woman in red maintains her strength and grace across all these spheres.

The art of multi-domain leadership isn't about perfect balance - it's about perfect presence. It's about bringing your full self to each role you inhabit, whether you're leading a board meeting or helping with homework. The skills that make us effective in one arena often translate seamlessly to another, though we don't always recognize this natural flow of leadership.

Consider how the patience developed in parenting enhances our ability to mentor team members, or how the strategic thinking required in professional settings can improve how we manage household dynamics. These crossovers aren't coincidental - they're the natural outcome of integrated leadership.

Heidi's story illustrates this beautifully. When faced with the simultaneous challenges of career promotion, a child's educational transition, and increased caregiving responsibilities for her ageing mother, she discovered that leadership principles transcend context. Rather than seeing these roles as competing forces, she recognized them as interconnected opportunities for growth and impact.

Her experience reflects what many women leaders discover: our various responsibilities don't divide our strength - they multiply our impact. Like the branches of a strong tree, each role we embrace adds to our stability rather than depleting it, provided we root ourselves deeply in proper self-care and clear boundaries.

As the woman in red, we must recognize that our leadership presence is needed everywhere we go. Whether in the boardroom or the living room, our ability to guide, inspire, and nurture makes a profound difference. The key lies not in compartmentalizing these different aspects of our lives, but in allowing them to enrich and inform each other.

This chapter explores how to harness your leadership capabilities across all domains of life while maintaining your vitality and effectiveness. We'll examine practical strategies for creating harmony between different areas of responsibility, building support systems that span multiple contexts, and ensuring that your leadership presence remains strong and sustainable across all spheres of influence.

Like the deep red of a sunset that bathes everything in its warm glow, your leadership influence has the power to transform every environment you enter. The question isn't whether you can lead in multiple domains - it's how to do so while maintaining your authenticity, effectiveness, and joy in the journey.

Harmonizing Home and Career: Strategies for Dual-Domain Leadership Excellence

The delicate art of harmonizing career and home life remains one of the most significant challenges facing women leaders today. Like the dual nature of fire, which both warms a home and powers industry, women must learn to channel their leadership energy effectively across both domains without depleting their inner flame.

Research consistently shows that women often shoulder a "double burden," managing both professional responsibilities and the majority of domestic duties[10]. However, this challenge presents an opportunity for women to demonstrate the unique strength of dual-domain leadership - the ability to nurture and guide across all spheres of influence.

Many women these days are senior executives battling between competing priorities of a demanding career and family responsibilities. Rather than viewing these domains as competing forces, the key to harmonizing home and career lies in intentional boundary management. Like the controlled burn of a skilled fire tender, successful women leaders establish clear parameters around their time and energy. This includes defining specific "off-hours" for family time and communicating these boundaries clearly to both colleagues and family members. The woman in red understands that boundaries aren't walls that separate - they're bridges that connect different aspects of life while maintaining necessary structure.

Strategic delegation becomes crucial in both domains. Just as a flame can be shared to light multiple torches without diminishing its own brightness, effective leaders distribute responsibilities thoughtfully. This might mean empowering team members at work while also engaging family members in household management. The goal isn't to do everything yourself but to orchestrate a harmonious flow of responsibilities across all domains.

Developing robust support systems is equally vital. Like the deep root system that nourishes a rose bush, women leaders need to cultivate networks that sustain them across all areas of life. This includes professional mentors, family support networks, and community resources. Research shows that women who build strong support systems report higher leadership sustainability and lower stress levels.

Integrative planning represents another crucial strategy. Rather than treating career and home as separate entities, successful leaders create synergistic approaches that allow for mutual enhancement. This might mean involving children in appropriate work projects to teach leadership skills or applying professional organization techniques to home management.

Flexibility and resilience remain essential qualities in this harmonization process. Like the adaptable nature of fire that can both warm a home and forge steel, women leaders must remain adaptable in response to changing demands[10]. This might mean adjusting work schedules to accommodate family milestones or reorganizing home routines to support crucial professional projects.

The practice of self-compassion cannot be overlooked in this journey. Just as a flame needs oxygen to sustain itself, women leaders must ensure they're nurturing their own well-being. This includes practicing self-care regularly, setting realistic expectations, and forgiving oneself for the inevitable imperfections in the balancing act.

Perhaps most importantly, women leaders must recognize that their dual-domain expertise represents a unique strength rather than a liability. The skills developed in managing a household - such as conflict resolution, resource allocation, and emotional intelligence - often translate powerfully into professional leadership contexts. Similarly, professional leadership skills can enhance family dynamics and personal relationships.

By embracing these strategies while maintaining clear boundaries and support systems, women can rise as powerful leaders across all domains of life. Like the woman in red who stands bold and unshakeable[10], they can create lasting impact both at home and in their careers, demonstrating that true leadership knows no boundaries - it simply adapts its flame to illuminate whatever space requires its light.

The Ripple Effect: Leveraging Leadership Skills Across Different Life Spheres

Like ripples expanding across a still pond from a single stone's impact, leadership skills cultivated in one area of life naturally extend their influence across all domains[2]. The woman in red understands that her leadership presence, like the warmth of a flame, naturally radiates outward, touching and transforming every sphere she inhabits. This ripple effect creates a powerful multiplier effect, where skills honed in one context enhance effectiveness in all others. The key is to ensure a seamless transition between domains to prevent burnout.

Research consistently shows that women who exercise leadership at home are more likely to pursue and excel in leadership roles outside the home, creating a virtuous cycle of growth and impact[2]. This comes in handy during interviews or when pitching a client. There is no excuse for a lack of experience, because everything you do in your home is a transferable leadership skill. Think about those moments when you stood in the kitchen trying to resolve World War III between your 9-year-old and 7-year-old. This is a major peacekeeping mission, and the skills harnessed from it are the art of conflict resolution, developed over years of family mediation, which will prove invaluable in managing complex organizational changes. Imagine the listening skills you develop and how you facilitate and navigate through tough conversations. These become a cornerstone of your professional success.

Leadership skills can indeed be transferred across domains, and this is not simply coincidental. The emotional intelligence required to guide a child through a crisis is the same muscles needed to mentor a struggling team member[2]. The strategic planning skills used to manage household resources translate directly to organizational budget management. Like the deep red roots of a mighty tree that nourish every branch, these core competencies strengthen our effectiveness across all spheres.

Consider how Indra Nooyi, former CEO of PepsiCo, often credited her early leadership experiences at home as foundational to her corporate success. She noted that "The skills I honed as a mother - listening, patience, and resilience - have been the bedrock of my success as a leader." This testament reinforces how leadership capabilities flow naturally between personal and professional domains.

The woman in red recognizes that her influence, like a controlled flame, can be intentionally directed to create positive change across multiple spheres. Whether mediating family disputes, driving organizational innovation, or advocating for community causes, the same core leadership principles apply: clear communication, emotional intelligence, strategic thinking, and purposeful action.

To effectively leverage this ripple effect, women leaders must first acknowledge the interconnectedness of their various roles. Rather than viewing family responsibilities, professional obligations, and community involvement as competing demands, they can be approached as complementary aspects of a unified leadership journey. Like the various facets of a ruby that catch and reflect light from different angles, each domain of leadership enriches and amplifies the others.

The key to maximizing this ripple effect lies in intentional reflection and strategic application. Regular self-assessment helps identify which skills are transferable and where growth opportunities exist[2]. For instance, the patience developed through mentoring junior colleagues might enhance one's approach to parenting teenagers, while the decisive action required in managing home crises could strengthen professional decision-making.

Michelle Obama's journey exemplifies this powerful ripple effect. Her leadership skills, initially honed in legal and executive roles, seamlessly translated into effective advocacy for education and health initiatives, demonstrating how leadership capabilities can create waves of positive change across multiple domains.

To harness this ripple effect, women leaders should:

- Regularly reflect on skills developed in one domain that could benefit others

- Seek opportunities to apply leadership strengths in new contexts

- Build support networks that span multiple life spheres[2]

- Practice intentional skill transfer between personal and professional domains

- Document successes and lessons learned across different leadership contexts

Like blood carrying vital nutrients throughout the body, leadership skills flow naturally across different spheres of life, nourishing and strengthening each area they touch. The woman in red understands that her leadership presence, like the steady flame of a torch, can illuminate multiple paths simultaneously.

By consciously cultivating and directing this ripple effect, women leaders can maximize their impact while maintaining authenticity across all domains. The key lies not in compartmentalizing different aspects of leadership, but in allowing them to flow naturally between spheres, creating waves of positive influence that extend far beyond their initial source.

Remember that each leadership moment, whether at home or in the boardroom, contributes to your overall growth as a leader. Like the embers of a fire that can ignite new flames, the skills and wisdom gained in one domain can spark transformation in others, creating an ever-expanding circle of influence and impact.

Building Your Support Ecosystem: Creating Sustainable Balance Across Domains

Just as a vibrant ecosystem in nature requires diverse elements working in harmony, a woman leader's support system must be intentionally cultivated across all domains of life. Like the intricate root system that nourishes a mighty red oak, your support ecosystem provides the foundation for sustainable growth in leadership and impact.

Harvard Business School research emphasizes that women, particularly women of color, face unique challenges in accessing effective networks and support structures [19]. However, like the resilient flame that grows stronger when properly tended, a well-designed support ecosystem enables women to thrive across all spheres of influence.

Women leaders must strive to build a carefully curated network of supporters across different life domains. Consider creating opportunities for regular check-ins with mentors who understand your unique challenges as a leader, or creating a family council for shared decision-making at home, and joining a community of women leaders who meet monthly for mutual support and growth.

The key to building a sustainable support ecosystem lies in recognizing that, as with the various properties of fire, different support serve different purposes. Professional mentors provide career guidance, while sponsors actively advocate for advancement opportunities[19]. Family members offer emotional sustenance, while community connections expand our sphere of influence.

To build your support ecosystem, consider these essential elements:

- Cultivate Authentic Networks: Develop relationships both within and outside your professional sphere[19]

- Establish Clear Boundaries: Like the controlled burn of a

skilled fire tender, set parameters that protect your energy

- Create Systems for Support: Implement practical structures that sustain balance across domains

- Nurture Reciprocal Relationships: Like the flow of blood that both gives and receives life-sustaining elements

- Practice Regular Self-Care: Maintain your inner flame through intentional restoration

Red School's research on women's leadership emphasizes that honoring self-care and natural cycles is vital for sustainable leadership[25]. Like the ebb and flow of a flame, women leaders must recognize when to surge forward and when to restore their energy.

Emotional intelligence plays a crucial role in building and maintaining your support ecosystem. Like the warmth of a steady flame that draws others near, your ability to understand and connect with others strengthens your network. Research shows that leaders who cultivate high emotional intelligence are more effective at building and sustaining supportive relationships[19].

Technology and flexible work arrangements can serve as powerful tools in your support ecosystem. Like the modern control systems that direct a flame's path, these resources help manage the flow of responsibilities and communication across different life domains.

Remember that your support ecosystem, like the deep red roots of a mighty tree, requires regular nurturing to remain strong and vital. Schedule regular check-ins with your support network, assess the effectiveness of your systems, and adjust as needed to maintain sustainable balance.

The woman in red understands that strength doesn't come from standing alone, but from building and maintaining robust support systems across all domains[26 27 28]. Like a flame that grows stronger when multiple embers join, your leadership capacity expands through the intentional cultivation of your support ecosystem.

By implementing these strategies while maintaining clear boundaries and authentic connections, you can create a support ecosystem that sustains your leadership across all domains of life. Like the woman in red who stands bold and unshakeable, you can build a network that empowers you to rise and thrive in every sphere of influence. As we conclude this chapter on navigating leadership across life's domains, let us remember that, like the deep red flame that burns most steadily when properly balanced, our leadership presence must be thoughtfully cultivated and maintained across all spheres of influence. The journey of the woman in red is not about perfect equilibrium, but about purposeful presence and impact in every domain she touches.

Remember that building a sustainable support ecosystem is not a sign of weakness, but a demonstration of wisdom. Like the intricate root system that anchors and nourishes a mighty tree, your network of support across domains strengthens your ability to stand tall and unshakeable. The woman in red understands that true strength comes not from bearing all burdens alone, but from creating systems and relationships that sustain her leadership across all areas of life.

As you move forward, continue to nurture your leadership presence intentionally across all domains. Let your flame burn bright in the boardroom and at the family dinner table. Allow your strength to manifest in both professional strategy sessions and quiet moments of maternal guidance. Remember that each domain of leadership - whether home, career, or community - adds another facet to your brilliance, like the many surfaces of a perfectly cut ruby.

Your journey as a woman in red is not about dividing yourself among competing demands, but about multiplying your impact through integrated leadership. Like the controlled flame that brings both warmth and light, your presence has the power to nurture and illuminate every space you enter. Continue to build your support systems, maintain clear boundaries, and remember that your leadership journey is not a sprint but a sustained flame that grows stronger with proper tending.

Step boldly into each domain of your life, knowing that the same strength that makes you an effective professional leader also makes you a powerful force for good in your family and community.

May you continue to rise as the woman in red, bold and unshakeable, bringing your unique light to every domain you touch.

Remember that your leadership journey is not about perfection, but about presence - showing up fully and authentically in every role you inhabit. As you move forward, may you find increasing harmony and impact across all domains of your life, creating a legacy of leadership that touches and transforms every life you encounter.

Reflection

List three leadership qualities developed through your home or community experiences that can be used in your professional leadership position.

Review

Make a Difference with Your Review

Unlock the Power of Generosity

"The best way to find yourself is to lose yourself in the service of others."
– Mahatma Gandhi

People who give expecting nothing in return often live happier and more fulfilled lives. So, let's make a difference together.

Would you help someone just like you, someone who desires to grow, lead, and step boldly into who they were created to be, but doesn't know where to begin?

My mission is to make **leadership, purpose, and personal growth simple, practical, and empowering for every woman.**

But to reach more women, I need your help.

Most people choose books based on reviews. Your words could

be the reason another woman finds the courage to rise, to believe again, and to walk boldly in her purpose.

Leaving a review costs nothing and takes less than a minute, but its impact can be powerful.

Your review could help...

...one more woman finds her voice.
...one more leader rises with confidence.
...one more mother leads her home with love and strength.
...one more entrepreneur steps into bold action.
...one more dream come alive.

The woman in red is a movement. And movements grow when we lift each other.

To make a difference, simply scan the QR code below and leave a review:

https://www.amazon.com/review/review-your-purchases/?asin=B0GX2QJMPV

https://www.amazon.co.uk/review/review-your-purchases/?asin=B0GX2QJMPV

If you believe in lifting others, encouraging growth, and helping women rise, then you are truly the woman in red.

Thank you sincerely.

Kemi Emmanuel

Chapter Six

Leading with Purpose: Decision-Making and Execution Excellence

Purpose, like the unwavering flame of a torch, illuminates the path through uncertainty and guides us toward decisive action even when fear whispers for retreat. In the dance between faith and fear, it is our connection to purpose that transforms hesitation into bold decision-making, much like how the deep red of dawn inevitably pushes back the darkness of night. The interplay between faith and fear in leadership creates a crucible where our greatest potential emerges. Like the refining process that transforms raw metal into precious gold, our leadership journey often requires us to face our deepest fears and transform them through unwavering faith in our purpose and capabilities.

As women leaders, we often find ourselves at crossroads where decisions carry significant weight - not just for ourselves, but for all those who depend on our leadership. These moments demand more than just analytical thinking or professional expertise; they require us to tap into a deeper well of wisdom that comes from aligning our actions with our core purpose and spiritual foundation.

The woman in red understands that purpose-driven leadership transcends traditional decision-making frameworks. She recognizes that while data and strategy play crucial roles, the most impactful decisions often emerge from deep inner knowing and spiritual alignment. Like the steady flame of a candle that remains unwavering even in turbulent winds, her leadership is anchored in something greater than circumstance.

The Woman in Red: Execution Excellence

The woman in red understands that excellence is never accidental; it is intentional, like the careful use of Chilli in a meal. Chilli is bold, vibrant, and unapologetically red; it doesn't hide, it defines the experience. In the same way, she brings spice to everything she does as a leader. She knows that without intention, even the most promising vision can fall flat. But when excellence is executed with purpose, it awakens something powerful in those around her. Just as Chilli transforms a dish, enhancing flavor, depth, and character, her leadership transforms environments, energizing people and elevating outcomes. Every decision she makes, every action she takes, is deliberate. She does not lead passively; she leads with precision, adding the right amount of "spice" at the right time. Because she understands this truth: execution excellence is not about doing more, but about doing what matters, with clarity, intention, and impact.

In this chapter, we'll explore how to harness the power of purpose-driven leadership while developing practical frameworks for decision-making and execution. We'll examine how faith can serve as a compass in uncertain times, guiding us toward choices that align with our deepest values and highest calling. You'll learn specific strategies for moving from analysis to action, ensuring that your decisions not only reflect your purpose but also translate into tangible impact.

The woman in red knows that true leadership excellence comes not from choosing between faith and strategy, but from integrating both into a powerful foundation for decision-making and execution. Like the deep crimson of a sunset that transforms the entire sky, her purpose-driven leadership has the power to transform not just her own path but the landscape of possibility for all those she serves.

The Woman in Red and The Power of Focus

Leading with purpose requires focus. Focus Like Blood in the Veins. The Woman in Red is like blood in the veins, direct, purposeful, and unwavering in her course. She knows that her life's work is to nourish, to bring oxygen, to strengthen what has been entrusted to her care.

Blood does not meander. It does not take detours. It flows with precision, carrying life to the organs that depend on it. And so must the Woman in Red. She focuses her energy on what truly matters, guarding her mission with the kind of determination that refuses to be scattered. In the body, blood flows steadily through the arteries and veins, delivering what is needed, where it is needed, at the right time. In leadership and in life, focus looks like clarity of vision, alignment with purpose, and a refusal to be distracted by noise.

When blood is contained within the vessels, life thrives. When we, as women and leaders, remain aligned to our calling, our families, teams, and communities thrive.

But when blood spills outside its pathway, through rupture, injury, or deviation, the result is damage. The organs starve. The body suffers. In the same way, when we allow distractions to pull us off course, those who depend on us suffer the consequences.

A leader who loses focus leaves her team wandering. A mother who abandons her post leaves her children uncertain. A woman who strays from her purpose leaves her community gasping for the oxygen she was meant to provide. Therefore the Woman in Red protects her focus as though her life depends on it, because in many ways, it does.

The Cost of Distraction

Distractions look harmless at first. It whispers promises of ease and detours dressed as opportunities. But when you say yes to everything, you dilute your power. Like blood spilling where it does not belong, distraction weakens your ability to deliver life where it truly matters.

Think of the many demands that call your name, endless responsibilities, competing expectations, and the pressure to compare yourself with others. Each one, if not filtered through a clear focus, can drain you. And when you are drained, you cannot give. The Woman in Red understands this. She says no, not out of pride, but out of wisdom. She says no to what pulls her off course, so she can say yes to what nourishes life.

Protecting Your Veins

Blood flows through protected channels, veins and arteries that safeguard its journey. For you, the channels are the structures, routines, and boundaries that hold you steady. Without them, purpose leaks away. The Woman in Red practices discipline. She carves out mindful moments to pause, reflect, and ask:

Am I still on course?

Is my energy directed where it gives life?

Am I nourishing what truly matters, or scattering myself where it doesn't?

These checkpoints keep her grounded. Like regular health checks for the body, they ensure that her leadership, motherhood, business, and calling remain infused with life.

The Purpose-Decision Matrix: Aligning Choices with Core Values and Vision

At the heart of every powerful leader lies a compass that guides decisions toward true north - their core purpose and values. Like the deep crimson threads that weave through a tapestry, creating both beauty and strength, our values and vision must be intricately woven into every choice we make. The Purpose-Decision Matrix emerges as a powerful tool for women leaders seeking to align their choices with their deepest convictions and highest aspirations.

This structured approach transforms the often-overwhelming process of decision-making into a clear, purpose-driven pathway. Like the steady flame of a torch that illuminates the darkness, the matrix helps us evaluate options against weighted criteria that reflect our most cherished values and boldest visions. It's not merely about making good decisions - it's about making decisions that fuel our purpose and advance our mission.

The matrix works by first identifying possible courses of action and the criteria most relevant to our vision and values. Each criterion is then weighed up based on its importance, often on a scale of 1-5[29] [30], ensuring that our most fundamental values carry appropriate influence in the final decision. This process transforms potentially ambiguous or emotionally charged decisions into clear, actionable outcomes grounded in measurable factors[31] [32].

Sometimes you might be facing a critical staffing decision during a period of budget constraints. Rather than allowing fear or external pressures to drive your choice, you develop a Purpose-Decision Matrix that weights criteria such as "patient care quality," "team well-being," and "long-term sustainability." By assigning higher weights to criteria that align with your core values, e.g., compassionate care and staff development, you can prioritize providing training and other programs over reducing staff numbers. This decision not only preserves team morale but also ultimately improves patient outcomes and departmental efficiency.

The power of the Purpose-Decision Matrix lies in its ability to link daily decisions with long-term purpose[32]. Like the deep roots that anchor and nourish a flourishing rose bush, our core values provide stability and sustenance for our leadership decisions. When we clearly articulate these values - whether they be integrity, empowerment, or inclusiveness - and translate them into specific decision criteria, we create a framework that ensures each choice supports our larger mission[32].

For the woman in red, this approach offers strength in overcoming fear-based decision-making. Just as a flame grows stronger when properly fueled, our confidence in decision-making grows when we know our choices are firmly grounded in our values and vision. The matrix provides objective support for bold decisions, helping us move beyond gut feelings or fear responses to choices that reflect our true calling[30][32][33].

Moreover, this framework creates transparency and builds trust with stakeholders. Like the warm glow of a fire that draws people together, a clear decision-making process invites understanding and participation from team members. It provides a documented record of how and why decisions were made, which is useful for reflection, learning, and defending choices when challenged [32].

However, we must remember that while the matrix is powerful, it isn't infallible. Not all qualitative factors can be easily scored, and developing the right criteria takes time and careful thought[33]. The woman in red understands that, like tending a fire, maintaining an effective decision matrix requires vigilance and periodic adjustment to ensure continued alignment with evolving values and vision[33].

To implement the Purpose-Decision Matrix in your leadership journey, begin by clearly defining your core values and vision. What principles are non-negotiable for you? What impact do you ultimately want to create? Translate these into specific criteria that can guide your decisions. Weight these criteria according to their importance in fulfilling your purpose[30][32]. Then, when facing decisions, evaluate each option against these weighted criteria.

Remember that this tool serves not just professional decisions but can guide choices across all domains of leadership - from family life to community involvement. Whether deciding on a new parenting approach or evaluating a community initiative, the matrix helps ensure your choices align with your deepest values and highest aspirations.

Like the transformative power of fire that refines gold, the Purpose-Decision Matrix purifies our decision-making, burning away doubt and uncertainty to reveal choices that truly reflect our purpose and values. In this way, we rise as women in red - bold, purposeful, and unshakeable in our leadership journey.

Faith-Fueled Leadership: Converting Fear into Strategic Action

Like a flame that transforms darkness into light, faith-fueled leadership can transmute our deepest fears into purposeful action. When we anchor our leadership in unwavering faith - whether spiritual conviction, profound purpose, or deep-seated values - we discover a wellspring of courage that transcends temporary anxieties and illuminates the path forward[16][18]. Just as the deep crimson of dawn inevitably pushes back the darkness, faith-fueled leadership dispels the shadows of doubt and hesitation.

Research in positive psychology reveals that leaders who connect their work to transcendent values and deeper meaning demonstrate greater resilience and effectiveness, particularly in high-pressure situations[18]. This scientific understanding affirms what many women leaders have discovered through experience - that faith provides not just comfort, but concrete strength for strategic action.

The woman in red understands that fear itself isn't the enemy - it's how we respond to it that matters[16]. Like the refining fire that transforms raw ore into precious metal, fear can serve as a catalyst for growth and strategic insight[16]. This transformation begins with acknowledging fear without shame, examining its root causes, and using it as data to inform rather than inhibit action.

For women leading in family contexts, faith-fueled leadership takes on additional dimensions[17]. A mother facing difficult decisions about her child's education or healthcare can draw upon the same principles: anchoring choices in core values, using fear as information rather than an obstacle, and taking strategic action aligned with deeper purpose. This could include prayer and meditation, committing decisions and actions to God, with reassurance that the Bible provides against fear.

The process of converting fear into strategic action involves several key practices[16 18]:

- Regular reflection on core values and purpose through journaling or meditation

- Visualization of positive outcomes while acknowledging potential challenges

- Building community with other faith-fueled leaders who provide support and accountability

- Developing clear decision-making frameworks aligned with foundational beliefs

Like the steady flame of a torch that remains unwavering even in strong winds, faith-fueled leadership provides stability in turbulent times. This stability comes not from the absence of fear, but from the presence of something stronger - an unshakeable conviction in our purpose and values[18].

The woman in red recognizes that leadership requires both inner work (anchored in spirituality) and outer action[34]. Just as a flame needs both fuel and oxygen to burn brightly, effective leadership requires both deep faith and strategic implementation. This dual focus allows us to move beyond reactive decision-making into purposeful, mission-driven action.

As Brené Brown wisely notes, "You can choose courage, or you can choose comfort, but you cannot choose both"[18]. Faith-fueled leadership doesn't eliminate discomfort - instead, it provides the courage to move forward despite it. Like the deep red roots that anchor and nourish a mighty oak, our faith provides the foundation from which bold action can spring.

In practical terms, this might mean starting each day with a purpose-centered ritual such as prayer or meditation, regularly assessing decisions against core values, or creating support systems that reinforce faith-based resilience[18]. The goal isn't to eliminate fear but to transform it - like the alchemist's fire that turns base metal into gold, faith transforms fear into fuel for strategic action.

The woman in red stands as a beacon of this transformative possibility[34]. Like the unwavering flame that both illuminates and warms, she demonstrates how faith-fueled leadership can light the way forward while inspiring others to find their own courage. Through this approach, we discover that our greatest fears often point the way to our most significant opportunities for impact and growth[16] [18]. We get the opportunity to learn from our fears and channel our actions to where they matter most.

Execution Excellence: Building Systems for Consistent Purpose-Driven Results

Like the precision of a master craftsman tempering steel, excellence in execution demands both artistry and systematic discipline. The woman in red understands that vision without implementation remains merely a dream, and purpose without process lacks the power to create lasting impact. Just as the steady flame of a well-tended fire requires both fuel and structure to burn consistently, sustainable results emerge from carefully designed systems aligned with our deepest purpose.

Research consistently shows that organizations and leaders who build purpose-driven systems significantly outperform their peers across multiple metrics, including innovation, employee engagement, and customer loyalty[3]. These systems serve as the foundation that transforms bold visions into tangible reality, much like how the deep roots of a rose bush enable its brilliant blooms to flourish season after season.

Consider the story of Indra Nooyi, former CEO of PepsiCo, who revolutionized her organization through what she called "Performance with Purpose." Like the unwavering flame that both illuminates and transforms, she redesigned PepsiCo's systems to align with a broader mission - delivering sustainable growth while being responsive to social and environmental needs. Her systematic approach to goal-setting, with clear metrics on both business and sustainability targets, demonstrated how purpose-driven execution can elevate an entire organization.

The woman in red recognizes that execution excellence requires three fundamental elements: clear purpose, systematic processes, and empowered teams[2]. Like the three legs of a tripod supporting a steady flame, each element is essential for sustainable success. She understands that systems should make the right thing the easy thing - removing friction and enabling purposeful action at every level.

In practical terms, this means establishing:

- Goal Setting and Cascading: Breaking down strategic priorities into clear, measurable objectives, including daily micro-objectives

- Feedback Mechanisms: Creating regular review cycles and open communication channels

- Standard Operating Procedures: Documenting essential processes for clarity and consistency

- Clear Decision Rights: Defining who has authority for specific choices

These systems extend beyond professional contexts into all domains of leadership. A mother implementing family routines that align with core values, a community leader establishing protocols for inclusive decision-making, or an entrepreneur creating scalable business processes - all benefit from systematic approaches to execution excellence.

As Rosabeth Moss Kanter wisely notes, "Leaders must wake people out of inertia. They must get people excited about something they've never seen before, something that does not yet exist." The woman in red embodies this principle, using systems not just for efficiency but as catalysts for transformation. Like the deep crimson of a rose that maintains its vibrancy through careful cultivation, excellence in execution requires ongoing attention and refinement.

This includes:

- Regular reflection and assessment of system effectiveness

- Continuous learning and adaptation based on feedback

- Celebration of progress and recognition of milestone achievements

- Integration of technology to streamline and enhance processes

The woman in red understands that execution excellence isn't about rigid control but about creating frameworks that enable consistent, purpose-driven results. Like the careful balance of a flame that provides both warmth and light, effective systems should support rather than stifle human potential.

Sheryl Sandberg emphasizes this principle in her observation that "Leadership is about making others better as a result of your presence and making sure that impact lasts in your absence." This sustainability - this ability to create lasting positive change - emerges from well-designed systems aligned with a clear purpose.

As you build your own systems for execution excellence, remember that creating and refining them will strengthen both your leadership and your organization. Start with a clear purpose, design with intention, and continuously refine based on results and feedback.

The woman in red knows that execution excellence is not a destination but a journey of continuous improvement. Like the eternal cycle of the flame that both consumes and creates, effective systems constantly evolve while remaining true to their core purpose. Through this disciplined approach to execution, she transforms bold visions into tangible reality, creating lasting impact that extends far beyond her immediate reach.

As we conclude this chapter on purpose-driven leadership and execution excellence, we're reminded that, like the steady flame of a torch, our leadership journey is both illuminating and transformative. The woman in red understands that the dance between faith and fear, between purpose and action, creates the unique rhythm of authentic leadership. Like the deep crimson of dawn that pushes back darkness, she knows that purpose-driven decisions have the power to transform not just individual moments, but entire trajectories.

Through our exploration of the Purpose-Decision Matrix, we've discovered that aligning choices with core values lays the foundation for bold, decisive action. We've seen how faith-fueled leadership transforms fear from an obstacle into a catalyst for growth. And we've learned that execution excellence requires both a systematic approach and spiritual alignment - like the careful balance of a flame that provides both warmth and light.

Like the refining fire that transforms raw ore into precious metal, the journey of purpose-driven leadership shapes us into more resilient, more authentic leaders. We learn that our greatest fears often point the way to our most significant opportunities for impact, and that systematic execution turns bold visions into tangible reality.

As you move forward in your leadership journey, remember that your purpose has the power to light the way not just for yourself, but for all those you lead. Whether you're making decisions in your professional role, guiding your family through transitions, or leading community initiatives, let your inner fire - your deep sense of purpose - be the compass that guides your choices.

The woman in red knows that leadership excellence isn't about perfection, but about consistent, purpose-driven action. Like the eternal cycle of the flame that both consumes and creates, effective leadership constantly develops while remaining true to its core purpose. Through this disciplined approach to faith-fueled, purpose-driven leadership, we create a lasting impact that extends far beyond our immediate reach.

May you go forth with renewed clarity about your purpose, confidence in your decision-making, and a commitment to execution excellence. Remember that, like the deep red roots that anchor and nourish a mighty oak, your faith and purpose provide the foundation from which bold, transformative leadership can flourish. The world needs your light - shine boldly, lead purposefully, and execute with excellence.

Action steps:-

Create your personal Purpose-Decision Matrix

Establish daily practices that strengthen your faith-fueled leadership

Design a new system for execution excellence in your area of influence

CHAPTER SEVEN

The Balanced Woman in Red: Self-Care, Value, Boundaries & Maximizing Impact

Like the steady flame of a well-tended fire, sustainable leadership requires a careful balance between giving of oneself and replenishing one's inner resources. The woman in red understands that her ability to illuminate others' paths depends on maintaining her own inner light through deliberate self-care, clear boundaries, and authentic empathy. The delicate art of sustainable leadership lies in mastering the dance between giving of ourselves and preserving our essence - much like the careful tending of a flame that must be neither smothered nor allowed to burn too intensely. For the woman in red, this balance isn't merely about time management or setting boundaries - it's about creating a sustainable legacy of impact while maintaining the vibrancy that makes her leadership uniquely powerful.

Like the measured breath of a seasoned practitioner, effective leadership requires rhythm - moments of intense engagement balanced with periods of restoration and reflection. The journey to mastering this balance often comes through hard-won wisdom.

Red as Fire: Passion with Boundaries

Fire has always captivated humanity. It warms, it lights, it protects, it cooks, it comforts. But left unchecked, fire can also burn, destroy, and consume everything in its path. Passion is the same. It is powerful, energizing, and transformative when contained, but dangerous when uncontrolled.

The Woman in Red knows the value of fire. She understands that passion fuels her purpose. It is the spark that ignites vision, the energy that sustains action, and the warmth that draws others near. But she also knows this truth: passion without boundaries can become a wildfire, leaving exhaustion and ashes in its wake.

The Power of Passion

Passion is the red flame in your heart that makes you rise early, persist when others quit, and keep going when the journey feels uphill. Without it, life becomes mechanical motions without meaning.

Passion attracts. Like a fireplace on a chilly night, it pulls people closer. Its glow inspires, its warmth comforts, its steady burn sustains. When you operate with passion, you create that same atmosphere.

The secret is that fire only sustains life when it's controlled. Walls are to a fireplace what glass is to a lantern, and structure is to a stove. To ensure passion is life-giving, not destructive, it needs boundaries, clear direction, and intentional focus.

Passion without boundaries leads to burnout. Passion with boundaries leads to brilliance.

The Danger of Burnout

Uncontained passion looks like over-committing. Saying yes to everything. Chasing every opportunity. Pouring out for everyone else while leaving yourself empty. Like fire spreading out of control, uncontained passion doesn't just drain you; it leaves behind ashes where fruit should be. The Woman in Red refuses to let her flame consume her. She watches for the early signs of burnout, fatigue, resentment, and disconnection, and pauses, replenishes, and protects her energy. She remembers that passion is not meant to drain her but to direct her.

Guarding the Flame

Boundaries are not barriers; they are safeguards. They do not restrict your passion; they protect it. The Woman in Red guards her flame with rhythms of rest, with the wisdom to say no, and with the discipline to focus on what matters. She does not apologize for these boundaries. She embraces them because she knows they keep her fire burning bright.

Boundaries are the walls that keep your fire alive, not the walls that keep you trapped.

She asks herself often:

- Where does my passion create warmth and value?

- Where am I spreading myself too thin?

- What practices keep my fire steady and strong?

Leading with Fire

When fire is contained, it can be shared. One flame can light a thousand candles without losing its own glow. Fire also spreads, burning everything in its wake. The Woman in Red uses her passion in the same way. She lights up her family, her team, her community, not recklessly, but intentionally. Her fire is not a wildfire; it's a guiding flame.

She knows when to glow, and when to step back to rest. She leads not by burning out, but by burning on.

A Call to Channel Your Fire

Your passion is your gift, your fuel, your flame. Guard it. Contain it. Direct it.

Don't let it scatter into burnout. Don't let it smoulder into nothingness. Use it to warm, to light, to inspire. Be the Woman in Red whose fire gives life, not ashes.

Fire without focus burns out. Fire with purpose lights the way.

The pursuit of balance isn't a sign of weakness, but a demonstration of profound leadership wisdom. Strategic self-care and boundary-setting can amplify rather than diminish our impact. It's a powerful testament to the truth that when we honor our own needs, we become better equipped to serve others.

The essence of sustainable leadership lies in understanding that our effectiveness isn't measured by the hours we work or the sacrifices we make, but by the lasting impact we create while maintaining our own well-being. Like the steady flame that burns neither too bright nor too dim, we must find our optimal state of energy and engagement.

As women who lead in multiple spheres - whether in healthcare, business, ministry, or family life - we often feel pulled in countless directions, each demanding our full attention and energy. The pressure to be everything to everyone can slowly dim our inner light if we don't intentionally protect and nurture it. This chapter will explore practical strategies for maintaining that delicate balance, ensuring that our leadership remains both powerful and sustainable.

We'll examine how to implement effective self-care practices that go beyond basic wellness routines to truly nurture our leadership capacity. We'll explore the art of setting boundaries that protect without isolation and discover how to cultivate empathy that enriches rather than depletes. Most importantly, we'll learn how to maximize our impact while ensuring our own flame continues to burn bright and steady.

The woman in red understands that her power lies not in constant sacrifice, but in sustainable strength. Like the enduring flame that provides both warmth and light, she knows that maintaining her own well-being isn't selfish - it's essential for those who depend on her leadership. Through intentional practices and strategic choices, she creates a legacy of balanced, effective leadership that inspires others to do the same.

The Self-Care Revolution: Strategies for Sustainable Leadership Energy

The journey to sustainable leadership energy begins with a revolutionary understanding: self-care isn't a luxury; it's a leadership imperative [36]. Like the carefully controlled flame that provides steady illumination, a leader must tend to her inner fire with intention and wisdom. This revolution in leadership thinking recognizes that our capacity to inspire, guide, and transform others is directly proportional to how well we nurture our own well-being.

The science of sustainable leadership energy reveals a profound truth: when women leaders prioritize self-care, they don't just survive - they thrive. Research from the Columbia University Women in Leadership program demonstrates that leaders who implement structured self-care practices show enhanced decision-making capabilities, improved team dynamics, and greater resilience when facing challenges [36].

Consider the metaphor of the red rose - it requires specific conditions to bloom: proper nutrition, adequate sunlight, and regular pruning. Similarly, sustainable leadership energy demands a holistic approach to self-care that encompasses physical, emotional, and spiritual well-being[36]. This isn't about occasional indulgence; it's about creating systematic practices that fuel our leadership fire.

The first pillar of the self-care revolution is physical wellness. Like the steady flow of oxygen that keeps a flame burning bright, our bodies require consistent care to maintain optimal leadership energy. This means prioritizing sleep hygiene, maintaining regular exercise routines, and ensuring proper nutrition - even during the busiest seasons of leadership[36].

Emotional intelligence forms the second pillar of sustainable leadership energy. Just as a flame must be protected from strong winds, our emotional well-being requires careful tending through mindfulness practices, regular reflection, and healthy boundary-setting[35]. The practice of emotional self-care allows us to remain responsive rather than reactive, maintaining our leadership presence even in challenging situations.

The third pillar focuses on mental clarity and psychological resilience. Like the focused beam of a lighthouse, our mental energy must be carefully directed and preserved. This involves implementing regular periods of deep work, interspersed with intentional breaks for mental recovery[36]. It means learning to say no to energy-draining activities that don't align with our core purpose.

Community support represents the fourth pillar of sustainable leadership energy. Just as multiple flames burn brighter together, women leaders thrive when connected to supportive networks[36]. This might involve regular mastermind sessions, mentorship relationships, or peer support groups where experiences and wisdom can be shared freely.

Practical strategies for implementing these pillars include:

- Creating morning and evening rituals that bookend your day with intentional self-care

- Establishing non-negotiable boundaries around your time and energy[35]

- Developing a personal energy audit system to assess and adjust your self-care practices regularly.

- Building a support network of fellow women leaders who understand your journey[36]

Like the woman in red who knows when to fan her flames and when to bank her fire, successful leaders must develop an intimate understanding of their energy patterns. This means recognizing the early warning signs of burnout and having systems in place to replenish energy before it's depleted.

The self-care revolution isn't about perfection - it's about progress. It's about understanding that our leadership impact is magnified, not diminished, when we prioritize our well-being. As Brené Brown reminds us, "You can't get to courage without rumbling with vulnerability."[35] This includes being vulnerable enough to acknowledge our need for rest, renewal, and rejuvenation.

By embracing the self-care revolution, we model sustainable leadership for the next generation of women leaders[35,36]. We demonstrate that true strength lies not in constant sacrifice, but in the wisdom to maintain our inner fire so it can continue to light the way for others. This is how the woman in red maintains her vibrant presence - not by burning herself out, but by tending to her flame with the same care and attention she gives to her leadership responsibilities.

Boundaries as Bridges: Setting Limits That Enhance Rather Than Restrict Impact

Like a well-tended garden that flourishes within its borders, effective leadership grows stronger through thoughtfully established boundaries. The woman in red understands that boundaries aren't walls that confine her influence but bridges that channel her energy toward meaningful impact - much like how the focused intensity of a flame creates more light than scattered sparks.[37,10]

Research from leading women's leadership programs reveals a profound truth: boundaries don't restrict our power - they amplify it. As noted in recent studies of successful female leaders, those who establish clear boundaries demonstrate greater resilience, sustained impact, and an enhanced ability to connect deeply with their teams[37]. Like the careful banking of a fire that allows it to burn longer and brighter, strategic boundary-setting enables leaders to maintain their effectiveness over time.

Consider the wisdom shared by Susan Ruskin, a distinguished dean and film producer, who emphasizes that maintaining clear boundaries is essential for preventing burnout: "Being able to maintain a clear sense of that horizon keeps you from allowing the burnout to trip you up along the way.... If you let people tip you off of that too easily, you will fail."[37] This insight reminds us that boundaries serve as guiding rails, directing our energy toward what matters most[10].

The art of setting boundaries that enhance rather than restrict requires three key elements:

- Clear articulation of core values and priorities[37]

- Transparent communication of limits[37]

- Consistent modeling of healthy boundaries for others[37]

Like the deep-red rose that thrives in its garden bed, our leadership flourishes when we create a protected space for growth and development. This means learning to say 'no' to demands that drain our energy without advancing our purpose, and 'yes' to opportunities that align with our vision and values[37].

Research on Black women leaders provides powerful evidence of how boundary-setting contributes to sustainable leadership. These leaders remain "poised and positioned for the day... perfectly prepared through years of expertise" precisely because they've learned to protect their energy and focus through strategic boundaries. They show "no wear and tear or fray around their edges" - a testament to the protective power of well-maintained boundaries[10].

Practical strategies for implementing boundaries that build bridges include:

- Establishing clear communication protocols that respect both your time and others'[37]

- Creating structured systems for delegation that empower team members while preserving your strategic focus[37]

- Developing rituals that protect your energy and maintain your leadership presence[37]

Like a controlled flame that provides steady illumination, boundaries help us maintain consistent energy for leadership across all domains, from professional responsibilities to family life. When we set boundaries with intention, we create space not just for our own growth but also for others to step into their strength[37].

The woman in red understands that boundaries aren't signs of weakness but demonstrations of wisdom[10]. Thoughtful boundaries channel our leadership energy where it can create the greatest impact. Through strategic boundary-setting, we build bridges of sustainable influence, creating pathways for others while preserving our own vitality[37][10].

Remember: boundaries don't diminish your light, they focus it. Like the carefully directed beam of a lighthouse that guides ships to safe harbor, well-maintained boundaries enable us to lead with greater clarity, purpose, and lasting impact[37]. In establishing these guiding principles, we create not walls that isolate, but bridges that connect our vision to reality, our purpose to impact, and our leadership to those we serve[37][10].

The Empathy Equation: Balancing Compassion with Personal Wellbeing

Like the steady flame that provides both warmth and light, empathy in leadership must be carefully balanced; too intense, and it can consume us; too dim, and it cannot illuminate the path for others. The woman in red understands that true empathy isn't about sacrificing her own well-being on the altar of others' needs, but about creating a sustainable flow of compassion that enriches both leader and follower.

I've learned from Harvard Business School's Advancing Women of Color in Leadership program that effective women leaders excel in emotional intelligence while maintaining clear boundaries that protect their vitality[19]. This delicate balance allows them to lead with both power and grace, much like the deep red rose, which offers beauty while protecting itself with thorns.

I love how Brené Brown, a renowned leadership researcher, puts it: "Empathy is the most important instrument in a leader's t oolbox."[35] However, like any powerful tool, it must be wielded with wisdom and intention. The woman in red recognizes that her capacity for empathy, like the flame she carries, requires careful tending to maintain its strength and effectiveness.

The strategic approach to balancing empathy involves three essential elements:

- Self-awareness and emotional intelligence practices that help us recognize our limits[19]

- Clear boundary setting that protects our energy while maintaining connection

- Intentional self-care rituals that replenish our capacity for compassion

Consider the wisdom shared in Will Power by Alexandra Pope and Sjanie Hugo Wurlitzer: "This world needs the full reinstatement of the Feminine for all life to flourish."[25] This flourishing requires us to honor both our natural inclination toward nurturing others and our own need for renewal.

Like the rhythmic flow of life-giving blood through our veins, sustainable empathy requires a continuous cycle of giving and replenishment. When we ignore this natural rhythm, we risk depleting our inner resources, leading to compassion fatigue and diminished leadership effectiveness[19].

Practical strategies for maintaining this vital balance include:

- Regular emotional check-ins to assess our capacity for engagement

- Establishing clear protocols for when and how we extend our emotional energy

- Creating sacred spaces in our schedules for personal renewal

The woman in red understands that her empathy, like her leadership presence, must be sustainable to be truly transformative. She recognizes the warning signs of emotional depletion and responds with the same care and attention she would offer others. This isn't selfishness - it's strategic wisdom that ensures her flame continues to provide light and warmth for those who need it most.

In the dance between giving and receiving, the woman in red maintains her balance through conscious choices and clear boundaries. She knows that true empathy doesn't require martyrdom, but it flourishes in the fertile soil of self-awareness and intentional care. Like the carefully banked fire that burns through the night, her compassion remains steady and sustainable, ready to warm those who approach while maintaining its essential strength.

The empathy equation isn't about perfect balance - it's about conscious choices that honor both our capacity for compassion and our need for renewal. When we master this delicate interplay, we create a leadership presence that, like the woman in red herself, remains both powerful and sustainable, capable of illuminating paths forward while maintaining its own vital flame. As we conclude this vital chapter on balance and sustainable leadership, let us remember that the woman in red, like a well-tended flame, derives her power not from burning bright and fast but from maintaining steady, sustainable illumination. Throughout this chapter, we've explored the delicate art of balancing self-care, boundaries, and empathy; essential elements that allow us to lead with both power and grace.

Like the deep crimson of a mature rose that has weathered many seasons, sustainable leadership requires both strength and flexibility. We need to learn that implementing structured self-care isn't a luxury but a strategic necessity and that intentional boundaries and self-care practices amplify, rather than diminish, our leadership impact.

The self-care revolution we've explored isn't about occasional indulgence; it's about creating systematic practices that fuel our leadership fire. Just as a flame requires proper conditions to burn steadily, our leadership energy demands consistent nurturing through physical wellness, emotional intelligence, mental clarity, and community support.

In examining boundaries as bridges, we've discovered that, like the banks of a river that direct its flow and amplify its power, thoughtful boundaries channel our leadership energy where it can create the greatest impact. These aren't walls that confine us, but guideposts that direct our influence most effectively.

Through the empathy equation, we've learned to balance compassion with personal well-being, understanding that our capacity to care for others must be matched by our commitment to self-renewal. Like the rhythmic flow of life-giving blood through our veins, sustainable empathy requires a continuous cycle of giving and replenishment.

As women who lead across multiple spheres; in healthcare, business, ministry, or family life, we must remember that our effectiveness isn't measured by the hours we work or the sacrifices we make, but by the lasting impact we create while maintaining our own wellbeing. The woman in red knows that her power lies not in constant sacrifice, but in sustainable strength.

I encourage you to implement the practical strategies we've explored: establish clear boundaries that enhance rather than restrict your impact, and maintain the delicate balance of empathy that allows you to lead with both heart and wisdom.

Remember, like the carefully controlled flame that provides steady illumination, your leadership light is meant to burn long and bright. By mastering the art of sustainable leadership, you ensure that your influence continues to illuminate paths forward while maintaining its own vital strength.

The woman in red isn't defined by constant motion or perpetual sacrifice, but by the wisdom to tend her inner fire so it burns steady and true. As you close this chapter, commit to honoring both your leadership calling and your need for renewal. For in this balance lies the secret to becoming truly unshakeable, a leader whose light not only illuminates the way for others but continues to burn bright and steady through all seasons of life. Like a well-tended rose, you learn to bloom through all seasons of life.

Your Voice is Oxygen

Whether you're a poet hiding your words in journals, a new businesswoman afraid to network, or a YouTuber considering quitting because you think no one's watching, you are needed. Your voice, your message, your presence, is oxygen to someone else's world. Sometimes we undervalue what we carry because we don't see the immediate results. But every time you show up boldly, you spark something in someone else. You remind them it's okay to be seen, to try, to fail, to rise, to shine. When you hold back, the world misses out.

Bold Leadership Begins With Bold Self-Belief

To be a woman in red is to be a woman who leads, not necessarily by title, but by presence. A woman who embodies transformational leadership, leading by example, empowering others, and leaving a legacy with every step.

She understands that leadership is not about perfection. It's about resilience, growth, and impact. And even if only one person is listening, that's enough to start a ripple effect.

Show Up with Purposeful Presence

Purposeful presence means choosing to show up as your true self. It's about authenticity over performance. When you are real, vulnerable, and intentional, people don't just hear you; they connect with you. Like the woman in red, you become magnetic. Your light, your energy, your fire, it spreads.

I, Kemi Emmanuel, believe in giving people a voice and living authentically. As a publishing strategist and coach, I give my full self to my clients to ensure they get their message across, share their stories, and reach the audience that needs them.

Whether you're launching a book, starting a new project, or trying to find your voice again, remember this:

You were never meant to blend in.

You were born to stand out.

Your Message Matters

So, to every woman reading this: wear your red. Not just in color, but in courage. Step up. Speak out. Stand strong. The world is waiting for your fire.

CHAPTER EIGHT

Divine Alignment: Spirituality as Your Leadership Foundation.

I've discovered that within every woman leader lies a wellspring of divine wisdom waiting to be accessed, a spiritual compass that guides decisions beyond mere logic and into the realm of inspired purpose. Like the unwavering flame of a sacred fire, spiritually-grounded leadership illuminates paths through uncertainty, transforming fear into faith-fueled action.

While spiritual seekers find guidance through prayer and meditation, today's women leaders are discovering that their greatest source of strength often comes from a deep connection to something greater than themselves. This understanding forms the cornerstone of spiritually grounded leadership, where faith becomes not just a personal practice but a transformative force that shapes how we lead, decide, and impact others.

In a world often driven by metrics and measurements, integrating spirituality into leadership might seem counterintuitive to some. However, research increasingly shows that leaders who maintain strong spiritual foundations often demonstrate greater resilience, clearer decision-making capabilities, and more authentic connections with their teams. The woman in red understands this profound truth - that like the deep crimson flame of a sacred candle, her leadership light burns brightest when fueled by divine purpose. As a Christian Minister, I have found that, through all seasons of pain and discomfort, my faith fuels my ability to lead with resilience and compassion.

Sometimes, when we find ourselves in a place where we must make major decisions that can change our life trajectory, fear can set in and derail sound decision-making. We must move from fear-based decision-making to faith-driven purpose. Like the dawn breaking through darkness, there must be the realization that leadership is a divine calling rather than merely a professional position, which illuminates the way for others seeking to integrate their spiritual foundation with their leadership practice.

This chapter explores how women can harness their spiritual intelligence to transform challenges into opportunities for growth and impact. We'll examine practical ways to develop a leadership style that draws strength from faith while maintaining professional excellence. By understanding the delicate balance between divine guidance and practical action, we'll discover how spiritual alignment can enhance, rather than diminish, our effectiveness as leaders.

As we journey through this chapter, we'll explore how the woman in red maintains her connection to divine purpose while navigating the complexities of modern leadership. Like the unwavering flame that burns bright regardless of external circumstances, spiritually-grounded leadership provides a steady source of wisdom, courage, and discernment. We'll learn how to access this inner wellspring of divine wisdom and transform it into tangible leadership practices that inspire and elevate those around us.

Integrating spirituality into leadership isn't about imposing religious beliefs on others, but about drawing from our deepest sources of wisdom and strength to lead with greater purpose and authenticity. Whether in healthcare, business, ministry, or family life, the principles we'll explore provide a foundation for leadership that transcends traditional boundaries and creates lasting positive impact.

Spiritual Intelligence in Leadership: Integrating Faith and Professional Excellence

Integrating spiritual intelligence into leadership represents a powerful fusion of inner wisdom and outward excellence, much like the deep red of a flame, which contains both light and heat. This dimension of leadership transcends traditional religious boundaries, offering a universal framework for leading with purpose, wisdom, and authenticity[39][41][42]. Like the woman in red, whose strength flows from both external preparation and internal conviction, spiritually intelligent leaders draw from a wellspring of divine wisdom while maintaining professional excellence.

It is imperative for women leaders to seek morning routines that require spiritual alignment, such as prayer and meditation. After all, the human body comprises the spirit, the soul, and the body. We are not just shells but living beings, led by our spirit. Just as nourishing our physical bodies is important, we must also learn to nourish our spiritual selves. A well-nourished spiritual leader leads from a place of peace and compassion rather than from harshness and stress. Asking God for divine wisdom to lead and make the right decisions is key to success and growth. We, humans, do not have the capacity to know everything.

Research by Yosi Amram reveals that spiritually intelligent leadership encompasses seven vital dimensions: meaning, grace, inner-direction, community, presence, truth, and wisdom[38][39]. These qualities, when cultivated intentionally, transform how we lead and influence others. Just as the red rose draws nutrients through its roots to manifest beauty in its blooms, spiritual intelligence nourishes leadership from the inside out.

Drawing upon spiritual intelligence to approach challenges holistically means creating space for morning reflection sessions. You could even encourage your team to gather and spend time in reflection in the mornings to voice concerns and find meaning in their work beyond metrics. By integrating compassionate listening with strategic planning, you can create an opportunity for team growth and a deeper sense of purpose.

Spiritual intelligence in leadership manifests differently across various life domains. In parenting, it might mean teaching children through presence and wisdom rather than mere authority. In healthcare leadership, it translates to treating patients and staff with grace while maintaining professional standards. As Cindy Wigglesworth notes, "Spiritual intelligence is the ability to behave with wisdom and compassion, while maintaining inner and outer peace, regardless of the situation"[41].

Like the woman in red whose presence illuminates paths for others, spiritually intelligent leaders inspire through embodied wisdom rather than positional power alone. Research demonstrates that teams led by such leaders experience higher engagement and productivity, with studies showing that inspired employees perform twice as effectively as those merely satisfied[38,40].

Developing spiritual intelligence as a leadership competency requires intentional practice. [38,39]. Consider these actionable strategies:

- Beginning each day with purposeful reflection, meditation, and prayer, connecting with your deeper values and vision

- Incorporate gratitude journaling into your morning or evening routine.

- Practice mindful presence in meetings and interactions, fully engaging with others

- Integrate gratitude practices into your leadership routine

- Create space for meaningful dialogue that goes beyond surface-level communication

- Approach challenges with both compassion and clarity

The woman in red understands that spiritual intelligence isn't about imposing beliefs but about accessing universal qualities of grace, wisdom, compassion, and purpose[39] [40]. Like the fire that both illuminates and transforms, spiritually intelligent leadership changes both the leader and those they lead. It provides a leadership foundation that remains unshakeable through challenges while maintaining the warmth of an authentic connection.

This might mean maintaining a calm presence during a crisis while making swift, rational decisions. In family life, it translates to leading with both strength and tenderness, creating spaces where growth and understanding can flourish. Integrating spiritual intelligence with professional excellence creates leadership that, like the woman in red, stands out not through force but through the natural radiance of purpose-driven wisdom.

As we navigate increasingly complex leadership landscapes, spiritual intelligence becomes not just an optional addition but a crucial foundation for sustainable success[38][39][40][41][42]. It enables leaders to move beyond fear-based decisions to faith-inspired action[39][41], transforming challenges into opportunities for growth and impact. Like deep-red embers that hold the potential for a renewed flame, spiritual intelligence provides an endless source of renewal and inspiration for the leader committed to excellence in all domains of life.

From Fear to Faith: Transforming Leadership Challenges Through Spiritual Principles

The journey from fear to faith marks a profound transformation in leadership, much like the metamorphosis of raw ore into precious gold through the refiner's fire. For women leaders, this transformation represents more than just overcoming anxiety; it embodies a spiritual awakening that turns challenges into catalysts for growth and impact. Faith becomes the force that transmutes fear into focused action and purposeful leadership.

Faith is believing positively even when results are not seen. It's the quiet conviction a leader has, through their spiritual belief in a higher being. Research consistently shows that women in leadership positions often face heightened levels of self-doubt and imposter syndrome. However, those who ground their leadership in spiritual principles demonstrate remarkable resilience and clarity of purpose. As Kim B. Clark notes, "The way to overcome fear and selfishness is to embrace the plan, embrace the grand plan of happiness fully and completely and seek to do the will of the Lord."[1] This spiritual perspective transforms leadership from a position of potential anxiety to one of divine calling and purpose.

When faced with implementing controversial new protocols, you might find yourself paralyzed by fear of criticism and potential failure. However, through daily spiritual practices of prayer and meditation, you can view your role not merely as an administrative position but as a sacred trust to improve client outcomes. This shift in perspective - from fear-based hesitation to faith-driven purpose - enables the implementation of necessary changes with both compassion and conviction. This can lead to renewed confidence, increased trust, and greater team engagement.

The transformation from fear to faith requires intentional practice and spiritual discipline. Like the woman in red, whose boldness emerges from inner conviction rather than external validation, leaders must cultivate specific spiritual habits that build faith and diminish fear[1]:

- Begin each day with purposeful prayer or meditation, connecting with divine guidance before engaging with challenges

- Practice gratitude journaling to maintain perspective during difficult situations

- Create regular moments of sacred pause throughout the

day for spiritual renewal

- Engage with supportive faith communities that nurture leadership growth

- Develop rituals that anchor decision-making in spiritual principles

In family leadership, this transformation becomes powerful. A mother facing tough decisions about her child's education or health care can draw upon spiritual principles to move from anxiety to confident action. The woman in red understands that her leadership role in the family, like her professional position, flows from a place of divine purpose rather than mere obligation[1].

The spiritual transformation of fear into faith also affects how we approach organizational challenges. Rather than viewing obstacles as threats, spiritually-grounded leaders see them as opportunities for divine intervention and growth. This perspective shift creates what research shows to be more resilient and effective leadership, particularly in crisis situations.

Like the deep red of dawn that inevitably pushes back the darkness, faith has the power to transform our leadership landscape. When we anchor our leadership in spiritual principles, we discover resources beyond our human limitations. The woman in red embodies this truth - she stands bold and unshakeable not because she never experiences fear, but because she has learned to transform that fear through faith into fuel for purposeful action[1].

This transformation requires both courage and vulnerability. It means acknowledging our fears while choosing to act from faith. It involves trusting in divine guidance while taking practical steps forward. Like the refiner's fire that produces pure gold, the process may be uncomfortable, but the result is leadership of lasting value and impact.

As we conclude this section, remember that the journey from fear to faith is not a one-time event but a continuous process of spiritual growth and leadership development. Each challenge becomes an opportunity to deepen our faith and strengthen our leadership impact. The woman in red understands this truth - like the eternal flame that both consumes and creates, her leadership continues to evolve through the transformative power of faith over fear[1].

Building a Divine Leadership Foundation: Daily Practices for Spiritual Alignment

The foundation of divine leadership, like the deep roots of a crimson rose, grows from daily practices that align our spiritual core with our leadership presence[25]. Just as the woman in red draws strength from both inner conviction and outward action, building a spiritual foundation requires intentional practices that connect us to our divine purpose while enhancing our leadership effectiveness.

Research consistently shows that leaders who maintain strong spiritual practices demonstrate greater resilience, clearer decision-making capabilities, and more authentic connections with their teams[16]. The integration of daily spiritual practices isn't about imposing religious beliefs but about cultivating a deeper connection to purpose and wisdom that enhances leadership effectiveness across all domains of life [25].

Why not practice starting each day with 20 minutes of mindful reflection before entering the work[6]. Combine this practice with regular breathing exercises between meetings and gratitude journaling. This can lead to profound transformation in your leadership style and, subsequently, the culture of your entire department. As a leader, you create a roadmap your team follows, and when you are grounded, you create a grounded team. You find your decisions become more balanced, your communication more compassionate, and your outcomes more positive.

The woman in red understands that spiritual alignment requires specific daily practices that nurture both inner wisdom and outer effectiveness[25]. Consider these foundational practices drawn from research in spiritual leadership:

- Begin each day with intentional quiet time for prayer, meditation, or reflection[16]

- Practice embodied awareness through movement, breathwork, or walking meditation[25]

- Maintain a spiritual journal to track insights, gratitude, and growth[16]

- Create regular moments of sacred pause throughout the day[25]

In family leadership, these practices take on special significance. A mother leading her household might begin each day with a moment of spiritual centering before waking her children, setting intentions for peaceful, purposeful parenting[25]. Throughout the day, she might practice brief moments of sacred pause, taking three deep breaths before responding to a challenging situation or expressing gratitude during family meals.

Like the deep red embers that hold potential for renewed flame, spiritual practices provide an endless source of renewal and inspiration[25]. They enable leaders to move beyond fear-based reactions to faith-inspired responses, transforming challenges into opportunities for growth and impact[16][25]. The woman in red embodies this truth - her leadership flame burns brightest when fueled by consistent spiritual practice.

Integrating spiritual practices into leadership requires both discipline and flexibility[25]. Just as the red rose follows natural cycles of blooming and rest, leaders must honor their own rhythms while maintaining consistent spiritual practices[25].

This might mean adjusting morning meditation times during busy seasons or finding creative ways to incorporate mindfulness into daily routines.

Research shows that leaders who maintain strong spiritual practices demonstrate improved decision-making, enhanced emotional intelligence, and greater resilience when facing challenges [16]. Like the refiner's fire that produces pure gold, these daily practices transform raw leadership potential into refined wisdom and effectiveness.

As we cultivate our divine leadership foundation through daily practices, we create not just stronger leaders but more authentic human beings[25].

The woman in red understands that her leadership impact flows from this deep well of spiritual alignment - like the sacred flame that both illuminates and transforms, her influence touches others through the natural radiance of purpose-driven wisdom[25]. As we conclude our exploration of spirituality as a leadership foundation, we return to the core truth that has illuminated this entire chapter: that, like the unwavering flame of a sacred fire, spiritually grounded leadership transforms both the leader and those they lead. The woman in red understands that her greatest strength flows not from external position or power, but from her deep connection to divine purpose and wisdom.

We have explored how spiritual alignment can transform fear into faith-driven action, creating leadership that remains steady even amid unprecedented change. We demonstrated that daily spiritual practices create the foundation for leadership that, like the deep red embers of a sacred fire, continues to provide warmth and light even through the darkest challenges.

Integrating spiritual intelligence with professional excellence creates leadership that stands out not through force but through the natural radiance of purpose-driven wisdom. Like the crimson rose that draws nourishment through its roots to manifest beauty in its blooms, spiritually-grounded leaders draw strength from both inner conviction and outward action.

As women leaders, we are called to more than just managing teams or achieving goals. We are invited into a deeper dimension of leadership that integrates faith with action, wisdom with decisiveness, and compassion with strength. The woman in red embodies this integration - she stands bold and unshakeable not because she never faces doubt, but because she has learned to transform challenges through faith into fuel for purposeful action.

Remember that building a divine leadership foundation is not a destination but a continuous journey of growth and transformation. Each challenge becomes an opportunity to deepen our faith, strengthen our impact, and illuminate paths for others. Like the eternal flame that both consumes and creates, our leadership continues to develop through the transformative power of spiritual alignment.

As you close this chapter, consider how you will begin implementing the practices and principles we've explored. Whether through morning meditation, gratitude journaling, or sacred pauses throughout your day, choose one or two practices to strengthen your spiritual foundation. Like the woman in red, whose presence naturally illuminates paths for others, let your leadership flow from authentic connection to divine purpose and wisdom.

The journey from fear to faith, from hesitation to bold action, from surface-level management to spiritually-grounded leadership - this is the path of the woman in red. May you continue to cultivate leadership that, like the deep crimson flame, both illuminates and transforms, creating a lasting impact in every domain of life you touch.

Reflection

What morning spiritual activity could you incorporate into your day moving forward?

CHAPTER NINE

Creating Your Leadership Tribe: Building Networks That Nurture and Lifting Others as You Rise

The most powerful leaders understand that genuine success isn't achieved in isolation, but through the intricate web of relationships we weave and nurture along our journey. Like the vibrant threads of a crimson tapestry, each connection in your leadership tribe adds strength, texture, and resilience to your professional fabric. Much like the threads of a tapestry gaining strength from their interconnection, successful leadership flourishes through the power of meaningful relationships and supportive networks. The journey of the woman in red isn't meant to be walked alone - her brilliance shines brightest when she ignites the potential in others while nurturing her own growth.

In the intricate dance of leadership development, building a strong support system becomes not just beneficial but essential. Like the steady flame that spreads from one candle to another without diminishing its own light, effective leaders understand that success multiplies when shared. They recognize that creating spaces for others to rise doesn't diminish their own power; it amplifies it.

As a mental health nurse and college principal-turned-entrepreneur, I have found that building a successful business requires a unique support system than the one developed in my regular job. As a practitioner who has helped countless individuals through their career transitions, I incorporated these skills into my business, but through a network of talented, experienced women who bring so much expertise and knowledge to our interactions.

Drawing from my previous experience and interactions, I approach networking differently, not as a task to complete, but as an opportunity to create meaningful connections. I created the Empowered Women Connect platform for women from ethnic minority backgrounds and the BLOOM summit to bring women together in ways that can help fuel their progress through meaningful interactions. As women, we must avoid the crab mentality of pulling each other down and instead see ourselves as a ladder to help each other up, regardless of our tribe or background. In doing this, we support each other's growth, and when we do, we see an exponential growth in our own businesses and well-being.

Through networking, we can find the guidance needed not only for our own businesses to thrive but also connections with key resources and mentors who help us elevate. My experience has taught me that building a leadership tribe isn't just about advancing my own journey - it is about creating a rising tide that lifts all boats, transforming individual success into collective triumph.

The woman in red understands that true leadership isn't measured by personal achievements alone, but by the trails she blazes for others to follow. Like the vibrant red rose that freely releases its fragrance, enriching its entire environment, she shares her wisdom, experiences, and connections generously. Her strength lies not just in her individual capabilities, but in her ability to weave together networks of support that sustain and elevate all who participate.

In this chapter, we'll explore how to build and nurture these vital connections, creating networks that both support your growth and enable you to lift others as you rise. We'll examine practical strategies for meaningful networking, mentorship dynamics, and the art of creating collaborative communities that foster collective success. Through understanding these principles, you'll learn how to transform your leadership journey from a solitary path into a powerful movement of mutual growth and empowerment.

Strategic Network Building: Creating and Nurturing Meaningful Professional Relationships

Like the steady flame that spreads from candle to candle, meaningful professional relationships illuminate paths to greater possibilities. The woman in red understands that her network is not merely a collection of contacts, but a vibrant tapestry of connections that, when woven with intention and care, creates a powerful foundation for collective growth and success.[43 44 45]

Strategic network building requires moving beyond superficial interactions to forge authentic, purposeful relationships.[43 45] Just as a single ember can ignite a powerful flame, each meaningful connection has the potential to spark transformative opportunities. Research shows that successful leaders master three distinct types of networking: operational networking within their immediate organization, personal networking for development and support, and strategic networking with influential individuals who help them realize long-term goals.[44 48]

Creating a lasting impact requires expanding your sphere of influence. A successful leader must endeavor to attend conferences, business networking meetings, and other opportunities for networking and interaction, not just as a participant but as an active connector, sharing her expertise while genuinely learning from others.[46] Like the deep red rose that releases its fragrance freely, enriching its entire environment, effective networking involves giving before receiving. This means sharing knowledge, making introductions, and offering support without immediate expectation of return.[45] As Michele Jennae wisely noted, "Networking is not about just connecting people. It's about connecting people with people, people with ideas, and people with opportunities."

To build a strategic network that nurtures and sustains leadership growth, consider these essential practices:

- Set clear, purposeful intentions for your networking goals, whether seeking mentorship, creating collaborative opportunities, or accessing new resources[48]

- Identify and target key connections aligned with your professional aspirations and values[46][48]

- Leverage multiple platforms, from professional associations to social media, for ongoing engagement[47]

- Practice authentic engagement through active listening and genuine interest in others[43][46]

- Maintain consistent follow-up to transform brief encounters into lasting relationships[43]

For women leaders, particularly those balancing multiple roles as professionals, parents, and community members, strategic networking takes on additional significance. Like the life-giving properties of blood that nourish every cell in the body, a well-cultivated network provides vital support, resources, and opportunities that sustain leadership across all domains of life.[44][46]

The power of strategic networking is exemplified by the success of initiatives like "Lean In Circles", which demonstrate how intentional relationship-building can create spaces for support, advocacy, and visibility for women leaders.[44] These networks serve as crucial counterbalances to traditional barriers, offering pathways for advancement and collective progress.

Just as fire requires oxygen to burn brightly, professional relationships need consistent nurturing to thrive. This means:

Maintaining organized records of contacts and interactions[47]

Scheduling regular check-ins with key network members

Creating opportunities for mutual support and collaboration[45]

Sharing successes and challenges openly to build trust

Celebrating and amplifying others' achievements

Remember that strategic networking isn't about collecting business cards or growing your social media connections. Like the carefully tended flame that provides both light and warmth, it's about cultivating relationships that enrich your leadership journey while creating opportunities for others to rise.[43] [45] Each connection in your network represents an opportunity not just for personal growth, but for collective advancement.

As the woman in red, your network becomes an extension of your leadership impact. Through thoughtful relationship building, you create pathways for others to follow, turning individual success into collective triumph. Like the ember that ignites new flames without diminishing its own light, your strategic network becomes a powerful force for transformation, illuminating possibilities not just for yourself, but for all those within your sphere of influence.[45]

The Mentorship Matrix: Both Receiving and Giving Guidance for Growth

Like the steady flame that guides others through darkness, mentorship illuminates paths to growth and transformation. The woman in red understands that true leadership involves both receiving light from those who've walked before and passing that flame forward to illuminate the way for others. This dual nature of mentorship - both receiving and giving guidance - creates a powerful matrix of growth that strengthens not just individuals, but entire communities of women leaders[19].

Mentorship, like the life-giving properties of blood flowing through veins, carries vital wisdom and support throughout professional networks. Research from Harvard Business School's Leadership Initiative demonstrates that women who engage in both sides of mentorship - as both mentee and mentor - accelerate their leadership development while creating a lasting impact in their organizations and communities[19].

We can transform our careers through the power of mentorship. Seeking guidance and mentorship early in our journey from established leaders in their fields is crucial, as is taking part in formal mentorship programs and cultivating informal relationships with other practitioners or entrepreneurs. We must reciprocate by extending the same support to others. The aim is to create a space where women can share challenges, celebrate victories, and grow together[35].

The mentorship matrix operates on several key levels that mirror the multifaceted nature of the woman in red:

- Receiving Guidance: Like the rose bud opening to receive sunlight, embracing mentorship requires vulnerability and openness to growth[19]

- Giving Support: As the flame spreads without diminishing, experienced leaders share wisdom while continuing their own development[19]

- Creating Legacy: Each mentoring relationship plants seeds for future generations of women leaders[19]

- Building Networks: Mentorship weaves stronger professional fabrics, creating resilient support systems[19]

- Fostering Innovation: Fresh perspectives flow between mentor and mentee, sparking creative solutions[19]

For the woman in red, mentorship becomes a powerful tool for both personal growth and collective advancement. As Brené Brown notes in "Dare to Lead," "Daring leaders who live into their values are never silent about hard things."[35] This truth applies especially to mentorship, where the authentic sharing of challenges and victories creates the foundation for genuine growth.

To maximize the benefits of the mentorship matrix, consider these strategic approaches:

- Seek diverse perspectives from multiple mentors across different areas of expertise[19]

- Create clear goals and expectations for mentoring relationships[19]

- Practice active listening and empathy in both receiving and giving guidance[19]

- Document insights and progress to track growth over time

- Celebrate successes and learn from challenges together

The power of mentorship extends beyond professional development into all aspects of life. Like the deep red of a sunset that transforms the entire sky, effective mentorship relationships often touch on personal growth, family balance, and spiritual development. This holistic approach ensures that leadership development aligns with authentic values and life purposes.

Research shows that organisations with robust mentorship cultures report higher levels of innovation, retention, and performance, particularly when women support each other's growth[19]. This ripple effect demonstrates how the woman in red's influence extends far beyond individual relationships, creating a lasting change in organizational cultures and professional communities.

Like the ember that ignites new flames without diminishing its own light, mentorship creates exponential impact through generations of leaders. Each woman who receives guidance and passes it on contributes to a growing network of support and empowerment[19]. This matrix of mentorship relationships becomes a powerful force for transformation, illuminating possibilities not just for individuals but for entire communities of aspiring leaders.

The mentorship matrix requires intentional cultivation and care. Just as a garden needs regular tending to flourish, mentoring relationships thrive through consistent attention and nurturing. This means:

- Scheduling regular check-ins and feedback sessions

- Creating safe spaces for vulnerable conversations

- Offering specific, actionable guidance while remaining open to learning

- Celebrating progress and acknowledging growth

- Adapting approaches based on changing needs and circumstances

Through the mentorship matrix, the woman in red not only accelerates her own growth but also creates a lasting impact by lifting others as she rises[19]. Like the steady flame that spreads from candle to candle, each mentoring relationship adds to the collective light of women's leadership, illuminating paths forward for generations to come[19].

Collective Rise: Strategies for Lifting Others While Advancing Your Own Leadership Journey

Like a vibrant flame that grows stronger as it spreads, collective leadership thrives on the principle of lifting others as it rises. The woman in red understands that her brilliance isn't diminished by igniting the potential in others - rather, like a magnificent bonfire, it grows more powerful through shared light and warmth. This transformative approach to leadership creates a legacy of empowerment that extends far beyond individual success.

Research consistently shows that women who actively cultivate strong professional networks, especially with other women, experience greater career satisfaction, higher promotion rates, and increased influence within their organizations10. The philosophy of "lift as you climb," coined by civil rights leader Mary Church Terrell, illuminates a powerful truth: our individual rise becomes more meaningful when we create pathways for others to follow.

Like the life-giving properties of blood that nourish every cell in the body, collective rise strategies should flow through every level of your leadership approach. Consider these essential practices:

Create intentional networks and supportive circles where individuals can share challenges and victories.

Move beyond mentorship to active sponsorship, using your influence to create opportunities for others

Share knowledge and resources transparently, ensuring information about opportunities reaches everyone

Celebrate and amplify the achievements of other women

Model inclusive leadership by practicing vulnerability alongside strength

The woman in red understands that true leadership power multiplies through sharing. Like the steady flame that ignites others without diminishing its own light, she creates spaces for collective growth and advancement. This approach transforms traditional hierarchical leadership into a collaborative journey of mutual empowerment.

The woman in red recognizes that leadership isn't a solo journey but a collective awakening[10]. Like the ember that ignites new flames without diminishing its own light, she understands that true power lies not in individual achievement but in the ability to create lasting change through collective advancement. Each woman she helps rise becomes another point of light in an ever-expanding constellation of leadership.

To implement collective rise strategies effectively, consider these practical approaches:

- Schedule regular networking meetings focused on opportunity sharing and problem-solving

- Develop a sponsorship mindset by actively championing

at least one emerging leader each year

- Create platforms for others to showcase their expertise and achievements

- Share your own challenges and learning moments to normalize growth and resilience

- Build coalitions across different backgrounds and experiences

Remember that collective rise isn't just about professional advancement - it extends into all aspects of life. Like the sunset that transforms the entire sky, effective leadership creates ripples of positive change throughout communities, families, and organizations. When women support each other's growth across all life domains, they create powerful networks of resilience and success.

The woman in red understands that her leadership journey is both personal and collective[10]. Like the fire that spreads warmth and light to all it touches, her influence grows stronger through sharing, support, and collective empowerment. By lifting others as she rises, she creates not just individual success stories but a lasting legacy of leadership that continues to illuminate paths forward for generations to come. As we conclude this chapter on building networks and lifting others, let us remember that, like the vibrant threads of a tapestry gaining strength from their interconnection, successful leadership flourishes through the power of meaningful relationships and supportive networks. The journey of the woman in red isn't meant to be walked alone - her brilliance shines brightest when she ignites the potential in others while nurturing her own growth.

Through our exploration of strategic networking, mentorship matrices, and collective rise strategies, we've discovered that true leadership power multiplies through sharing. Like the steady flame that spreads from candle to candle without diminishing its original light, each connection we forge, each person we mentor, and each opportunity we create for others adds to our collective strength and impact.

Let us carry forward the understanding that building our leadership tribe isn't just about advancing our own journey - it's about creating rising tides that lift all boats. Like the deep red rose that freely releases its fragrance, enriching its entire environment, we must share our wisdom, experiences, and connections generously. Our strength lies not just in our individual capabilities but in our ability to weave together networks of support that sustain and elevate all who participate.

Remember that as the woman in red, your network becomes an extension of your leadership impact. Through thoughtful relationship building and intentional mentoring, you create pathways for others to follow, turning individual success into collective triumph. Like the life-giving properties of blood that nourish every cell in the body, your leadership tribe provides vital support, resources, and opportunities that sustain growth across all domains of life.

As you step into the next chapter, commit to being both flame and fuel in your leadership community. Create spaces where others can shine, amplify voices that need to be heard, and build bridges that connect aspiring leaders to new opportunities. For in the end, your legacy as a leader will be measured not just by your personal achievements, but by the trails you've blazed for others to follow.

Like the ember that ignites new flames without diminishing its own light, may your leadership continue to illuminate paths forward, creating lasting impact through the power of connection, mentorship, and collective rise. For this is the way of the woman in red - bold enough to lead, wise enough to learn, and generous enough to lift others as she rises.

Reflection

Who currently makes up my leadership tribe, and in what ways are they contributing to my growth, or limiting it?

How intentionally am I nurturing my other relationships, and am I giving as much value as I am seeking?

In what practical ways am I lifting other women as I rise, and where can I do more?

CHAPTER TEN

Shaping Tomorrow, building a legacy

Legacy isn't measured in moments but in the ripples of impact that continue long after we've moved on, like the lasting glow of a sunset that transforms the entire sky. Just as a single flame can ignite countless others without diminishing its own light, true leadership creates endless possibilities that extend far beyond our immediate reach. As we conclude our journey through the dimensions of bold, unshakable leadership, this final chapter invites us to cast our vision beyond the present moment and into the legacy we're creating. Like the radiant glow of a sunset that paints tomorrow's promise across today's sky, our leadership journey isn't complete until we've created pathways for others to rise.

The art of legacy building requires us to think beyond individual achievement to consider the lasting impact we leave for future generations. Just as a single red thread can strengthen an entire tapestry, each action we take today weaves into the fabric of tomorrow's possibilities. This chapter explores how women leaders can architect sustainable systems of success, mentor rising leaders, and create lasting change that echoes through generations.

Legacy answers the question: How do you want to be remembered? I remember when I first started writing; I did a LinkedIn write-up about this. I didn't realize how this would transform my life. Over 30 books later, I really lived what I spoke about. I have left a legacy as an award-winning author.

Would you like to be remembered?

Not just for what you did, but for what you overcame, who you helped, and the legacy you left behind?

Would you prefer to be a fleeting butterfly, here today and forgotten tomorrow? Or would you rather be etched in history, like Roald Dahl, Charles Dickens, Barbara Cartland, Joan Collins, or Frederick Forsyth, writers whose words continue to inspire generations?

On the day of your funeral, people may speak highly of you. But what remains the next day, the next year, the next generation? That's why your story matters. Legacy is not about being famous. Legacy is about being remembered. Remembered for your strength, your faith, your journey, your truth. If the writers of the Bible had kept their experiences to themselves, what wisdom would we have lost?

Imagine a world with no history. No guideposts. No stories of hope through adversity. As a woman in red, your life is a message. And someone needs to hear it.

Like the deep red rose that releases its seeds to create new gardens of possibility, true leadership involves planting the seeds of future success. In this chapter, we'll explore how to create sustainable systems that outlive our direct influence, how to mentor effectively across generations, and how to build frameworks that support continuous growth and innovation. We'll examine practical strategies for succession planning, knowledge transfer, and creating opportunities for others to rise while maintaining our own growth trajectory.

The woman in red understands that her fire isn't meant to burn in isolation; - it ignites other flames, creating a constellation of light that illuminates paths for generations to come. As we delve into this final chapter, we'll discover how to transform our leadership journey from a solo expedition into a legacy that creates endless possibilities for others to rise, shine, and lead with their own unique brilliance.

Legacy Building: Creating Sustainable Impact Through Strategic Leadership

Creating a lasting legacy requires the same careful attention as tending to a sacred flame - it must be nurtured consistently, shared strategically, and protected thoughtfully to ensure its light continues to illuminate future generations. Like the deep crimson of a sunset that transforms the entire sky, true legacy-building leadership creates ripples of impact that extend far beyond our immediate reach, touching lives we may never meet but whose paths are forever brightened by the trails we blaze. As an author, I was in awe the first time I saw my book purchased by someone in India, Canada, the United States, and even countries I had never even heard of. I felt I was touching the lives of people whose paths I would never cross.

This taught me that strategic legacy building begins with understanding, and our leadership journey isn't just about personal achievement - it's about creating sustainable systems and cultures that empower others to rise[1]. As women in red, we are required to think beyond individual success and consider how our influence can create lasting positive change.

It is important to remember that demonstrating true legacy isn't about maintaining the status quo - it's about creating fertile ground for continuous growth and innovation.

Like the deep red rose that releases its seeds to create new gardens of possibility, strategic legacy building involves planting the seeds of future success through:

- Establishing robust mentorship programs that create clear pathways for advancement

- Developing systems and processes that can adapt and grow beyond our direct influence

- Creating cultures of innovation where new ideas are welcomed and nurtured

- Building strong networks that support and elevate women leaders at all levels

- Documenting and sharing wisdom in ways that can be easily accessed and implemented by others

The woman in red understands that her fire isn't meant to burn in isolation - it ignites other flames, creating a constellation of light that illuminates paths for generations to come1. She recognizes that true legacy-building requires both courage and humility: the courage to lead boldly and create change, and the humility to know that our greatest achievements often come from empowering others to surpass us.

Strategic legacy building also means considering how our leadership affects all spheres of influence - from professional environments to family life and community engagement. Just as blood carries vital nutrients throughout the body, our leadership legacy should nourish and strengthen every area it touches. This might mean creating family traditions that teach leadership principles to our children, establishing community programs that empower other women, or developing professional initiatives that create opportunities for leaders across multiple generations.

The most powerful legacies are built on a foundation of values that stand the test of time1. Like the unwavering flame that guides travelers home, these core principles provide direction and inspiration long after specific programs or initiatives have evolved. They remind us that legacy building isn't just about what we achieve - it's about who we become and who we empower others to be.

As we consider our own legacy, we must ask ourselves: How can our leadership today create ladders of opportunity for tomorrow? What systems and cultures are we establishing that will continue to grow and adapt beyond our direct influence? How are we ensuring that the light we carry ignites other flames that will burn bright long after we've moved on to new horizons?

Remember, the woman in red doesn't just climb to the top - she creates pathways for others to follow2, illuminating the way with her wisdom, strengthening others with her support, and ensuring that her impact continues to ripple outward in ever-widening circles of influence and possibility.

The Ladder Effect: Developing Systems for Generational Success

The concept of the Ladder Effect in leadership is much like the way a flame passes from one torch to another - it illuminates not just the immediate path but creates a chain of light that extends far into the future. Just as the deep roots of a mighty tree nourish every branch and produce seeds for future forests, effective leadership systems must nurture current growth while planting the seeds of tomorrow's success. It is necessary for us, as leaders, to build a ladder mentality, where we stand as ladders to help others grow, and, in doing so, we leave a legacy. This is the opposite of crab mentality, which drags others down.

Systemic leadership development begins with a robust foundation, much like blood carrying vital nutrients throughout the body to sustain life. Research shows that successful leadership programs incorporate assessment-based approaches, combining personalization, coaching, and continuous feedback to ensure skills are not just taught but deeply embedded 16. These systems, like the steady flame of a torch, must be carefully tended and passed on to ensure their light continues to illuminate paths for generations to come.

Like the deep crimson heart of a rose that nurtures its outer petals to bloom, effective leadership development systems must include:

- Structured assessment and feedback mechanisms that identify both strengths and growth areas16

- Mentorship and sponsorship programs that create clear pathways for advancement

- Institutional support systems that foster innovation and resilience16

- Documentation and knowledge-sharing platforms that preserve and transmit wisdom

- Cultural transformation initiatives that prioritize inclusivity and continuous learning

The woman in red understands that true legacy building requires thinking in systems - considering how decisions, policies, and cultures influence not just today's leaders but tomorrow's as well. This systems thinking approach, championed by thought leaders like Peter Senge[18,] ensures that the ladders we build are sturdy, scalable, and sustainable.

Historical figures like Anita Garibaldi demonstrate how individual courage combined with systemic action can create generational change. Despite operating in environments where women's participation was often discouraged[34,27,] she established essential support systems and inspired countless others to step into leadership roles[34,27,26.] Her story reminds us that the ladders we build today must be strong enough to support those who will climb them tomorrow.

The Ladder Effect also extends beyond professional environments into family life and community engagement. Just as blood carries life-giving oxygen throughout the body, leadership development systems should nourish and strengthen every area they touch. This might mean creating family traditions that teach leadership principles to children, establishing community programs that empower other women, or developing professional initiatives that create opportunities for leaders across multiple generations.

Like the unwavering flame that guides travelers home, effective leadership development systems must be built on a foundation of timeless values while remaining adaptable to changing circumstances. They should incorporate both the wisdom of experience and the innovation of new perspectives, creating a dynamic framework that grows while maintaining its core strength.

The woman in red recognizes that her leadership journey isn't just about reaching new heights - it's about creating sustainable pathways for others to follow. She understands that genuine success isn't measured by personal achievements alone, but by the strength and accessibility of the ladders she builds for future generations. Through intentional system building and careful nurturing of emerging leaders, she ensures that her flame ignites a constellation of lights that will continue to illuminate paths long after she has moved on to new horizons.

Infinite Horizons: Expanding Leadership Impact Beyond Traditional Boundaries

Like a flame that spreads its warmth beyond the confines of its hearth, true leadership knows no boundaries. The woman in red understands that her influence, like the deep crimson of a sunset, has the power to transform entire horizons, painting new possibilities across the canvas of tomorrow. On this journey to expand leadership impact, we discover that the most profound changes often come when we dare to look beyond traditional limits. We find that a single spark can ignite a forest of possibilities.

The landscape of women's leadership is booming, with contemporary leaders moving beyond established paradigms to influence systems, cultures, and industries on a global scale10. Just as blood carries vital nutrients throughout the entire body, effective leadership must flow freely across artificial boundaries, nourishing every part of the system it touches. This expansion requires both vision and courage - the vision to see beyond current limitations and the courage to step into uncharted territory.

- Expanding leadership horizons requires strategic approaches that combine vision with practical action:

- Cultivate systems thinking that recognizes interconnections across industries and culture

- Build sustainable networks that transcend organizational boundaries

- Create innovative platforms for knowledge sharing and collaboration

- Develop mentorship programs that reach beyond traditional professional sectors

- Establish cross-cultural initiatives that embrace diverse perspectives

The woman in red understands that true impact often requires challenging conventional wisdom. Like the deep roots of a mighty tree that extend far beyond its visible canopy, her influence must reach into unexpected spaces, nurturing growth in areas others might overlook. This might mean bringing leadership principles into family dynamics, introducing innovative practices in traditional settings, or creating new pathways for others to follow.

Studies on women's leadership reveal that those who successfully expand their impact often demonstrate remarkable resilience and adaptability10. They understand that leadership, like the unwavering flame of a torch, must remain steady even as it illuminates new territories. This resilience enables them to transform obstacles into opportunities, using challenges as catalysts for broader systemic change.

Consider how Anita Garibaldi's influence transcended geographical and cultural boundaries, demonstrating that leadership impact knows no limits. Her journey from rural Brazil to shaping revolutionary movements across continents shows how women leaders can create lasting change that extends far beyond their immediate sphere of influence.[26][27][2]

The woman in red recognizes that expanding leadership horizons isn't just about reaching new heights - it's about creating new possibilities for others to soar. Like the life-giving properties of blood that nurture every cell it touches, her leadership must enrich and empower every life it encounters. This might mean:

Establishing mentorship programs that cross generational and cultural boundaries

- Creating innovative platforms for knowledge sharing and collaboration

- Building bridges between different sectors and communities

- Developing new models of leadership that embrace diversity and inclusion

- Fostering environments where others feel empowered to expand their own horizons

Expanding leadership impact requires a delicate balance between vision and action, much like the careful tending of a sacred flame. It demands that we remain grounded in our core values while reaching beyond our comfort zones. The woman in red understands that true leadership legacy isn't measured by the height of her own achievements, but by how far her influence extends in creating positive change for others.

As we conclude this exploration of infinite horizons, remember that your leadership journey, like the endless expanse of the sky at sunset, knows no bounds. Your impact, like the warmth of a flame, can spread far beyond its origin, igniting new possibilities and illuminating paths for generations to come. The question isn't how high you can climb, but how many others you can lift as you rise, creating a constellation of leadership that brightens the entire horizon of possibility. As we conclude our exploration of legacy building and infinite horizons, let us remember that like the deep crimson sunset that paints tomorrow's promise across today's sky, our leadership journey is both a destination and a beginning.

The woman in red understands that true legacy isn't measured in individual achievements, but in the constellations of light we ignite in others.

Through this chapter, we've discovered that building a legacy requires both the fierce determination of fire and the nurturing flow of lifeblood. We've learned that sustainable impact comes not from standing alone at the summit but from creating sturdy ladders that enable others to climb. Like the deep red rose that releases its seeds to create new gardens of possibility, our leadership must plant the seeds of future success while maintaining our own growth and vitality.

Leadership Legacy is the knowledge we leave behind through our actions. It is no longer trendy to stay in your own corner and keep your knowledge, experience, and skills to yourself. No matter where you find yourself, as a woman, you are a natural-born leader, and a leader leads. You just need to harness that internal flame and cause its fire to affect future generations.

The journey of the woman in red teaches us that leadership knows no boundaries - it flows through every aspect of life, from the boardroom to the living room, from community spaces to sacred places. Just as blood carries vital nutrients to every part of the body, true leadership nourishes and strengthens all it touches. Whether you're guiding your team through organizational change, mentoring rising leaders, or creating pathways for your children to develop their own leadership abilities, your influence creates ripples that extend far beyond your immediate reach.

Remember that, like the refining fire that transforms raw materials into precious gold, every challenge you face is an opportunity to emerge stronger, more resilient, and better equipped to light the way for others. Your leadership journey isn't just about reaching new heights - it's about creating sustainable pathways for generations to come.

As you close this chapter and reflect on your own leadership legacy, consider how your flame can ignite others, how your wisdom can create ladders of opportunity, and how your influence can expand beyond traditional boundaries. The woman in red doesn't just climb to the top - she creates new summits for others to reach.

Your leadership story is still being written, and like the endless expanse of a crimson sunset, its potential knows no bounds. Continue to burn bright, to lift as you climb, and to create pathways that will illuminate the journey for countless others. For in the end, our greatest legacy isn't in the heights we reach alone, but in the constellation of leaders we inspire to rise, shine, and transform their own worlds with the bold, unshakeable spirit of the woman in red.

Reflections

What do I want to be remembered for beyond my achievements? What impact do I want to leave behind?

How am I documenting, sharing, or preserving my story, wisdom, and experiences for future generations?

If my leadership journey ended today, what legacy would remain and what needs to change?

CHAPTER ELEVEN
Conclusion

As we draw this transformative journey to a close, let us remember that the woman in red isn't just a metaphor - she is the embodiment of every woman who dares to rise, lead, and create a lasting impact in her sphere of influence. Like the multifaceted symbolism of red itself, she represents life, passion, boldness, and the fire that refines gold to its purest form.

Throughout this book, we've explored how true leadership emerges from within, shaped by the fires of challenge and strengthened by purposeful action. We've seen how the woman in red navigates the delicate balance between strength and vulnerability, between professional excellence and personal well-being, between leading others and nurturing herself. From the foundations of emotional intelligence to the heights of spiritual alignment, we've discovered that authentic leadership requires both inner transformation and outer manifestation.

The journey of leadership is not a solitary path but one enriched by the connections we forge and the lives we touch along the way. As you step into your full power as a woman in red, remember that your influence extends far beyond your immediate circle. Each bold decision, each boundary set, each act of authentic leadership creates ripples that impact generations to come.

The principles and strategies shared in these pages are not just theoretical concepts - they are practical tools forged in the real-world experiences of women who have dared to lead with purpose and passion. Whether you're leading in the boardroom, the emergency room, the classroom, or the home, these insights will continue to guide you as you navigate your unique leadership journey.

As you close this book, know that this is not an ending but a beginning. The woman in red within you has always been there, waiting to emerge in her full glory. Like the dawn that breaks through darkness, your leadership light should shine brightly, illuminating paths for others while staying true to your authentic self.

Remember that leadership is not about perfection but about progress, not about having all the answers but about having the courage to ask the right questions. It's about being refined by challenges rather than defined by them. As you step forward in your leadership journey, carry with you the strength of the woman in red - bold, resilient, purposeful, and alive with possibility.

Let your leadership be a testament to the power of authentic influence, where success is measured not just in personal achievements but in the lives you've touched and the leaders you've inspired. Like the vivid red of a sunset that paints the sky with possibility, may your leadership create beautiful horizons of opportunity for generations to come.

You are the woman in red - bold, beautiful, and burning bright with purpose. Rise unafraid, lead with heart, and let your light illuminate the way for others. Your time is now, and your impact knows no bounds. Stand tall in your truth, walk boldly in your purpose, and never forget that within you lies the power to transform not just your own life but the lives of countless others.

The world needs your leadership, your voice, and your unique contribution. Step forward with confidence, knowing that you are equipped, empowered, and called to make a difference. The woman in red is ready to rise - and that woman is you.

Kemi Emmanuel

About the author

Kemi Emmanuel

Kemi Emmanuel is a distinguished British multi-genre author, publisher, educator, coach, speaker, mental health nurse, minister, and entrepreneur. With a passion for personal development and a commitment to empowering individuals across various spheres of life, Kemi has dedicated her career to creating transformative experiences that foster growth in careers, businesses, relationships, mental health, finances, and emotional well-being. She has been a leader in academia, business, ministry, mental health,over twenty and in her family.

Literary Contributions Kemi is the acclaimed author of over thirty impactful books, including:

• Money Skills for Teens Made Simple: A practical guide aimed at equipping young individuals with essential financial literacy skills.
• Love Made This Happen: A heartfelt exploration of love's transformative power in relationships.
• Muna and Her Superhero Hair: A children's book celebrating self-identity and confidence.
• Manifesting Purpose: A motivational work guiding readers toward discovering and fulfilling their life's purpose.

Her diverse bibliography reflects her commitment to addressing the needs of various audiences, from children and teens to young and adult readers, providing resources that inspire and educate.

Professional Endeavors besides her writing, Kemi is a seasoned educator and coach, leveraging her expertise to mentor individuals in personal and professional development. Her background as a mental health nurse and practitioner informs her holistic approach to well-being, emphasizing the interconnectedness of mental, emotional, and spiritual health.

As a minister, Kemi integrates faith-based principles into her work, offering guidance that resonates with individuals seeking purpose and direction. Her entrepreneurial ventures further demonstrate her dedication to creating platforms that support growth and transformation.

As the founder of Kemi Emmanuel Publishing, she empowers

individuals to heal, grow, and share their message by helping them publish their books. As a mental health professional, coach, and businesswoman, she is passionate about helping others turn pain into purpose and ideas into impact.

Also by

KEMI EMMANUEL

Author Page: amazon.com/author/kemiemmanuel

Author Page: amazon.co.uk/author/kemiemmanuel

GROWING IN GOD'S LOVE
Stories to Teach Biblical Principles
Growing in God's Love
A beautifully illustrated Christian storybook that introduces children to God's love through gentle Bible-based lessons, kindness, and faith.
A Meaningful Gift That Grows With Your Child

SHADOWS OF TWO WORLDS
A Gripping Cross-Cultural Family Drama of Secrets, Betrayal, and Redemption
KEMI EMMANUEL

BIBLE WORD SEARCH AND ACTIVITY
BOOK FOR ADULTS AND TEENS

Author Page: amazon.com/author/kemiemmanuel

Review

Keeping the Movement Alive

Now you have everything you need to **become a bold, unshakable, and alive** leader; it's time to share what you've gained and help another woman rise.

By simply leaving your honest review of this book on Amazon, you become part of something bigger. You help other women, just like you find the courage, clarity, and confidence they've been searching for.

Your words can guide a woman who feels stuck.
Your voice can encourage a woman who is ready to rise.
Your experience can light the way for someone still finding hers.

This is how the movement grows.
This is how the woman in red multiplies.

When you leave a review, you're not just sharing an opinion—you're passing forward purpose, strength, and bold leadership.

Thank you for being part of this journey. Thank you for choosing to rise. And thank you for helping another woman do the same.

The flame of **bold leadership** stays alive when we share what we've learned, and today, you are helping to keep it burning.

 Click here to leave your review on Amazon.

https://www.amazon.com/review/review-your-purchases/?asin=B0GX2QJMPV

https://www.amazon.co.uk/review/review-your-purchases/?asin=B0GX2QJMPV

CHAPTER TWELVE
Bibliography

References

1 Clark, K. B.. (2018, March 20). *Embrace the Plan*. BYU Speeches. https://speeches.byu.edu/talks/kim-b-clark/embrace-the-plan/

2 Giovinazzo, D.. (2021, August 03). *The Woman in Red*. Book shop.org. https://bookshop.org/p/books/the-woman-in-red-dia na-giovinazzo/14619663

3 Fabiani, L.. (2009, September 1). *Library of Clean Reads*. Library of Clean Reads. http://www.libraryofcleanreads.com/2020/06/

4 WorkForce Institute. (2025, March 11). *The Neuroscience of Leadership: How Women Harness Emotional Intelligence for Success*. WorkForce Institute. https://workforceinstitute.io/women-i

n-leadership/neuroscience-of-women-in-leadership/

5 Andrew, L. & Andrew, E.. (2023). *Designed to Lead: The Female Brain and Leadership*. ACSA Content. https://content.acsa.org/designed-to-lead-the-female-brain-and-leadership/

6 Mumble Forum. (2023, November 15). *Unlocking the Power of Neuroplasticity: Building Strong Leadership Skills*. Mumble Forum. https://www.mumbleforum.com/post/unlocking-the-power-of-neuroplasticity-building-strong-leadership-skills-1

7 Muselman, C.. (2025, March 24). *The Neuroscience of Gender and Leadership: How Biology and Psychology Shape Leadership Styles*. WorkersCompensation.com. https://www.workerscompensation.com/daily-headlines/the-neuroscience-of-gender-and-leadership-how-biology-and-psychology-shape-leadership-styles/

8 Anderson, W. L.. (2025, March 25). *The Impact of Neuroscience on Leadership Development*. Leadership Science Institute. https://www.leadershipscienceinstitute.com/the-impact-of-neuroscience-on-leadership-development/

9 The Mind Solution. (2024, December 17). *Why Nervous System Regulation Is the Missing Link for Women in Leadership*. The Mind Solution. https://www.themindsolution.com/blog/Why-Nervous-System-Regulation-Is-the-Missing-Link-in-Leadership

10 Allen, A.. (2020, December). *The Black Woman's Math Problem: Exploring the Resilience of Black Women Who Lead in*

the United States Federal Government. Journal of African American Studies. https://go.gale.com/ps/i.do?id=GALE%7CA640859526&sid=googleScholar&v=2.1&it=r&linkaccess=abs&issn=15591646&p=AONE&sw=w

11 Landry, L.. (2019, April 03). *Why Emotional Intelligence Is Important in Leadership*. Harvard Business School Online. https://online.hbs.edu/blog/post/emotional-intelligence-in-leadership

12 Holistique Training. (2023, August 23). *The 4 Pillars of Emotional Intelligence and Why They Matter in 2025*. Holistique Training. https://holistiquetraining.com/en/news/elevate-relationships-through-emotional-intelligence-a-guide-to-lasting-bonds

13 Daniel Goleman. (2023, July). *EI Overview: The Four Domains and Twelve Competencies*. Daniel Goleman Emotional Intelligence. https://danielgolemanemotionalintelligence.com/ei-overview-the-four-domains-and-twelve-competencies/

14 Schosser, A.. (2023, March 30). *What is Emotional Intelligence?*. Retorio. https://www.retorio.com/blog/what-emotional-intelligence

15 Ceruto, S.. (2024). *Pillars of Emotional Intelligence: Mastering the 4 Key Components*. MindLAB Neuroscience. https://mindlabneuroscience.com/pillars-of-emotional-intelligence/

16 The Leadership Challenge. (2025, September 26). *Unleash the Leader Within*. The Leadership Challenge. https://www.leaders

hipchallenge.com/home

17 Nirupama P.R.V.. (2017, August 16). *Leadership & Management Books for Women, By Women.* Goodreads. https://www.goodreads.com/list/show/114693.LeadershipManagementBooksforWomenByWomen

18 Garry J.. (2016, May). *10 Books Every Nonprofit Leader Should Read.* Joan Garry Consulting. https://joangarry.com/nonprofit-leadership-books/

19 Harvard Business School Executive Education. (2024, January 15). *Advancing Women of Color in Leadership.* Harvard Business School Executive Education. https://www.exed.hbs.edu/advancing-women-color-leadership

20 International Trademark Association. (2024, March 8). *The Women's LeadershIP Initiative.* International Trademark Association. https://www.inta.org/about/our-commitment-to-women-in-ip/

21 Golin. (2022, July 27). *Golin Launches Executive Impact Matrix.* Golin APAC. https://golin.com/apac/2022/07/27/golin-launches-executive-impact-matrix/

22 Leader Navigation. (2024, March 14). *Measuring Leadership Impact.* Leader Navigation. https://www.leadernavigation.com/measuring-leadership-impact-2/

23 Meridian Team. (2023, December 16). *The Matrix of Lead-*

ership: A Guide to Transformative Influence. Meridian University. https://meridianuniversity.edu/content/the-matrix-of-leadership-a-guide-to-transformative-influence

24 Ashmore J. A.. (2024, August 14). *The Mayo Leadership Impact Index Adapted for Matrix Leadership Structures: Initial Validity Evidence*. Journal of Healthcare Leadership. https://pmc.ncbi.nlm.nih.gov/articles/PMC11330859/

25 Red School. (2024, January 15). *Menstruality is the feminine path to leadership*. Red School. https://www.redschool.net/for-leaders

26 Giovinazzo, D.. (2021, August 03). *The Woman in Red*. Barnes & Noble. https://www.barnesandnoble.com/w/the-woman-in-red-diana-giovinazzo/1135269451

27 Giovinazzo, D.. (2020, August). *The Woman in Red*. Reading Group Choices. https://readinggroupchoices.com/books/woman-in-red-2020/

28 Giovinazzo, D.. (2021, August 3). *The Woman in Red*. Grand Central Publishing. https://www.grandcentralpublishing.com/titles/diana-giovinazzo/the-woman-in-red/9781538717431/

29 Gaudet, C.. (2025, April). *Decision Matrix Framework: How Agency Leaders Make Faster, Better Decisions*. Predictable Profits. https://predictableprofits.com/decision-matrix-framework-how-agency-leaders-make-faster-better-decisions/

30 King, G.. (2024, December 18). *Decision matrix overview: benefits, examples and applications*. Pip Decks. https://pipdecks.com/blogs/leadership/decision-matrix-overview

31 Peek, S.. (2024, January 13). *What Is a Decision Matrix? Definition and Examples*. Business News Daily. https://www.businessnewsdaily.com/6146-decision-matrix.html

32 Spears, M.. (2023, March 8). *Prioritizing with a decision matrix*. Simplifying Processes. https://www.simplifyingprocesses.com/blog/prioritizing-with-a-decision-matrix

33 Meegle. (2025, August 26). *Decision Matrix Pros And Cons*. Meegle. https://www.meegle.com/en_us/topics/decision-matrix/decision-matrix-pros-and-cons

34 Kachuba, J.. (2020, August). *The Woman in Red*. Historical Novel Society. https://historicalnovelsociety.org/reviews/the-woman-in-red/

35 Career Contessa Team. (2023, December 12). *The 18 Best Leadership Books for Women*. Career Contessa. https://www.careercontessa.com/advice/leadership-books/

36 Columbia Business School Executive Education. (2024, February 01). *Women in Leadership: Next Level Success*. Columbia Business School Executive Education. https://execed.business.columbia.edu/programs/wil

37 Kramer, R. & Madden, C.. (2013). *The Artist as Leader: Susan*

Ruskin. UNC School of the Arts. https://www.uncsa.edu/kenan/artist-as-leader/susan-ruskin.aspx

38 Intelligensi. (2019, September). *Spiritually Intelligent Leadership (SILeadership™)*. Intelligensi. https://intelligensi.com/spiritually-intelligent-leadership/

39 Sherman, B.. (2024, January 15). *Leading with Soul: The Power of Spiritual Intelligence | Yosi Amram | 589*. Thought Leadership Leverage. https://thoughtleadershipleverage.com/the-power-of-spiritual-intelligence-yosi-amram/

40 Amram Y.. (2023, December). *Cultivate spiritual intelligence as a leader to inspire and empower*. SmartBrief. https://www.smartbrief.com/original/cultivate-spiritual-intelligence-as-a-leader-to-inspire-and-empower

41 MacFarlane, K.. (2020, October). *Leadership and Spiritual Intelligence : An introduction – Part 1*. Kathy MacFarlane. https://kathymacfarlane.com/leadership-and-spiritual-intelligence-an-introduction-part-1/

42 Griffiths, R.. (2016, June). *Definition of Spiritual Intelligence*. SQI.co. https://sqi.co/definition-of-spiritual-intelligence/

43 Golden, G.. (2023, June 2). *3 types of networking all successful people must master*. Gail Golden Consulting. https://www.gailgoldenconsulting.com/insights/3-types-of-networking

44 Leybeck, T.. (2024, September 06). *Networking 101: Building*

professional connections in business. Thunderbird School of Global Management. https://thunderbird.asu.edu/thought-leadership/insights/networking-101

45 Cochran, Cochran, and Yale. (2024, April). *Strategic Networking: Building Connections for Executive Success*. Cochran, Cochran, and Yale. https://ccy.com/strategic-networking-building-connections-for-executive-success/

46 Indeed Editorial Team. (2025, June 6). *8 Effective Networking Strategies for Professionals*. Indeed. https://www.indeed.com/career-advice/career-development/networking-strategies

47 Exline, E.. (2023, December 5). *5 ways to strategically build your professional network*. University of Phoenix. https://www.phoenix.edu/blog/strategic-networking-why-it-pays-to-plan.html